The Chase Organics Gardening Manual

Chris Algar

LONDON

IAN ALLAN LTD

DEDICATION

To my wife who does much
of the gardening, posed for
many of the photographs in
this book and who is
available for TV
appearances.

*All photographs reproduced in
this book were taken by
Chris and Anne Algar.*

*Line drawings by
Dick Armstrong.*

First published 1989

ISBN 0 7110 1861 8

Published by Ian Allan Ltd,
Shepperton, Surrey; and printed
by Ian Allan Printing Ltd at their
works at Coombelands in
Runnymede, England

Contents

1 Why Grow Organically?

Below:
Part of the Henry Doubleday Research Association's organic gardening display at Ryton Gardens.

My interest in gardening really began in the early 1970s when I moved to my present address and took over a very overgrown garden. Fortunately, one of the first books on the subject that I borrowed from the library was written by Lawrence Hills of the Henry Doubleday Research Association (HDRA), an organic gardening society. Being very impressed by the book, I cultivated the garden organically from the beginning. Experience of growing vegetables in my garden and allotment, which I took on in 1982, has convinced me that an organic system can really work.

Since I began gardening, there has been increased public awareness about the dangers of polluting the environment and contaminating foodstuffs. Many factors may have contributed to this increased public concern, but I feel sure that acid rain, disasters at chemical plants and an exploding nuclear power station must have played their part. Organic gardening and farming have much to offer people who wish to reduce pollution in food and in the countryside.

Although any form of cultivation, by definition, is unnatural, the organic approach is to work with rather than against natural processes whenever possible. A simple change in growing conditions, instead of a poisonous spray, may be used to overcome many of the problems encountered in gardening. As an example, a few years ago I began to have trouble with grey mould on greenhouse tomatoes. Originally, no ventilation was provided around the lower part of the greenhouse and this meant that the circulation of air was greatly restricted, unless the door was left open. Instead of spraying against the mould, I removed a small panel in the door to allow fresh air to enter the greenhouse, and have not been troubled by the disease since.

I have already used the term 'organic system' and would like to emphasise that the various techniques employed are to some extent interdependent. A mulch, for instance, used for excluding the light from no-dig potatoes, will also reduce evaporation of water from the soil, restrict weed growth and add organic matter to the soil when it finally decays. If I were cynical, I could also point out an example of interdependence in inorganic gardening where excessive use of nitrates can lead to soft growth, subsequent pest attack and inevitable spraying. There is evidence to suggest that excessive amounts of nitrate fertilisers used in agriculture lead to increased levels in the water supply and in crops, and this does not seem to be a good thing in view of the possible health risks involved.

The chemical warfare sections to be found in many garden centres are so extensive that newcomers to gardening could be excused for thinking that no plant could survive without such protection. The names of the products seem to be chosen not

for any scientific meaning, but for their emotional appeal to people who wish to turn their gardens into battlegrounds. The range of products is extensive even gardeners who wish to kill off their earthworms are catered for. There are a number of objections to pesticides, the most notable of which are: danger to human health, toxicity to beneficial insects and other forms of wildlife, the production of resistant strains of pests, and cost. Judging just how safe these products are is not easy because there may not be agreement among researchers, and a compound that is on sale in one country may be banned in another. Some chemicals which were previously thought of as safe have since been banned and so one may well ask how many of those now on sale will be considered dangerous in the future.

I apologise for starting off the book with such a seemingly negative attitude, but consider it reasonable to give an explanation of why I believe the organic approach to gardening is so important. The chapter has been kept short because the aim of this book is not to cover the shortcomings of garden chemicals in detail. Instead, I have described various techniques of organic gardening which should make their use unnecessary and the question of their safety irrelevant for the gardener.

Far left:
The bottom panel of the greenhouse door has been removed for extra ventilation.

Left:
Beneficial insects such as bees . . .

Below:
. . . and hoverflies can be harmed by spraying.

2 A Fertile Soil

Below:
Worm casts are an indication of a fertile soil.

When changing over to organic gardening from a more conventional form of cultivation, it is necessary to adopt a completely new approach; it is not simply a matter of swapping chemical fertilisers and pesticides for organic alternatives on a one-for-one basis. This point can be illustrated by the different ways in which orthodox and organic growers view their soil. The conventional method of supplying plant foods is by the application of soluble fertilisers. These chemicals bypass the biological activity of the soil, are available all at once and may be easily lost by leaching. Excessive amounts of such fertilisers can disturb the balance in the soil, causing trace elements to become unavailable and subsequent mineral deficiencies in plants. The organic approach, on the other hand, is to regard the biological activity in the soil as vitally important. Instead of feeding plants directly with chemicals, the organic gardener relies on the minerals already in the soil being made available by plant root secretions and the action of soil micro-organisms.

The complex relationships that exist among animals, plants and soil micro-organisms allows the recycling of nutrients to take place. Plants take minerals from the soil, they are eaten by animals, and then animal waste is turned back into plant food by bacteria and fungi. This process maintained the fertility of soils for a very long time without the use of fertilisers. In the modern world, one difficulty involved in attaining such a closed cycle is caused by the loss of nutrients in sewage. Contamination of some sewage sludge with heavy metals renders it unsuitable for use on the land. On a garden scale, recycling waste plant material via the compost heap will keep losses to a minimum and the plant foods contained in brought-in manures will help to replace those removed by crops. On soils where there is a deficiency of a particular mineral, this can be put right by the use of a slow-acting fertiliser such as rock phosphate.

Below:
A sample of soil is shaken with chemicals from the kit . . .

Right:
. . . and the colour of the resulting liquid is compared with a chart.

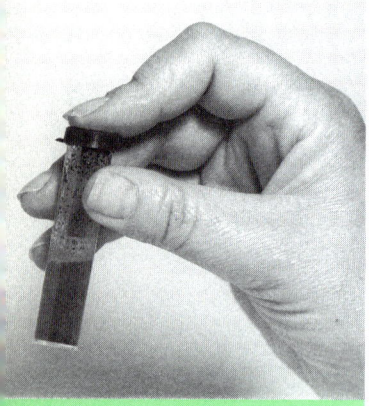

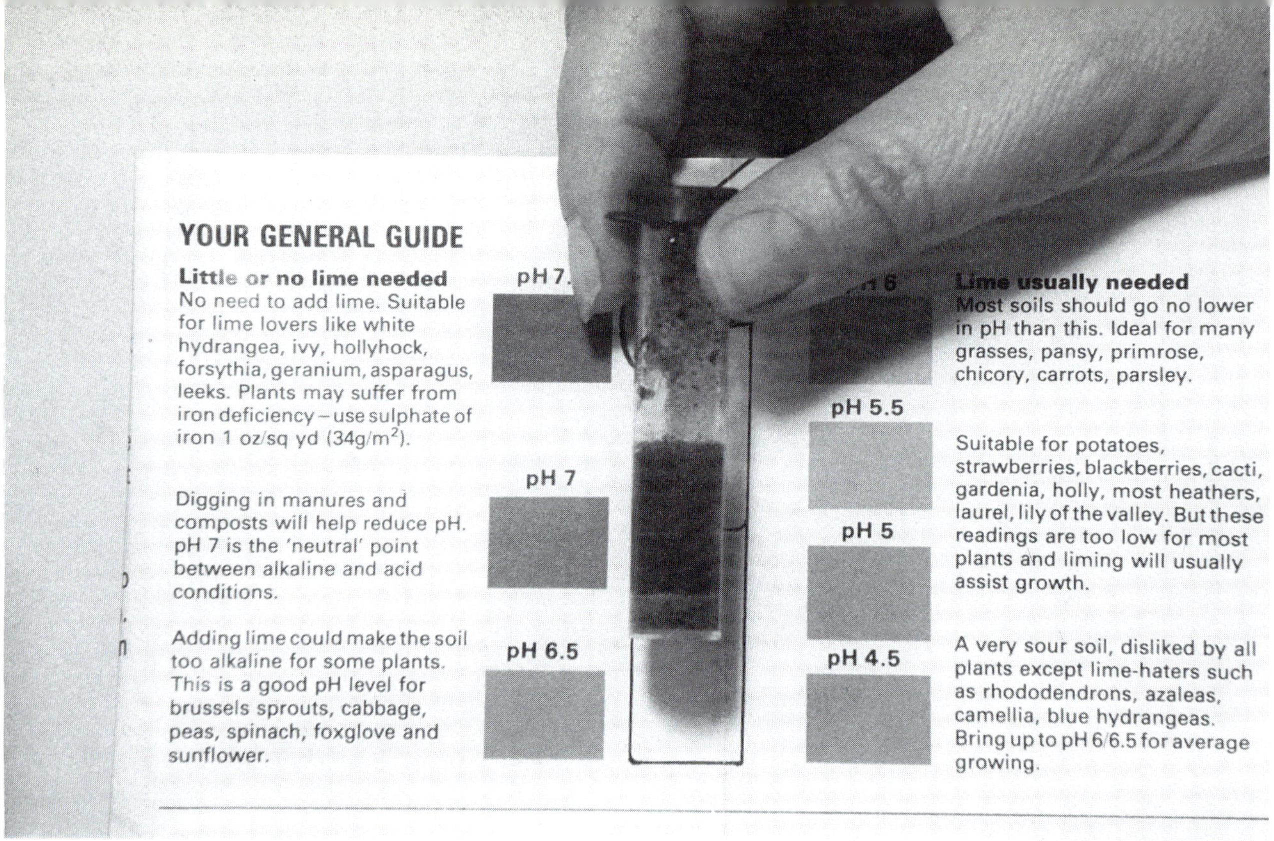

YOUR GENERAL GUIDE

Little or no lime needed
No need to add lime. Suitable for lime lovers like white hydrangea, ivy, hollyhock, forsythia, geranium, asparagus, leeks. Plants may suffer from iron deficiency – use sulphate of iron 1 oz/sq yd ($34g/m^2$).

Digging in manures and composts will help reduce pH. pH 7 is the 'neutral' point between alkaline and acid conditions.

Adding lime could make the soil too alkaline for some plants. This is a good pH level for brussels sprouts, cabbage, peas, spinach, foxglove and sunflower.

pH 7.

pH 7

pH 6.5

1 6

pH 5.5

pH 5

pH 4.5

Lime usually needed
Most soils should go no lower in pH than this. Ideal for many grasses, pansy, primrose, chicory, carrots, parsley.

Suitable for potatoes, strawberries, blackberries, cacti, gardenia, holly, most heathers, laurel, lily of the valley. But these readings are too low for most plants and liming will usually assist growth.

A very sour soil, disliked by all plants except lime-haters such as rhododendrons, azaleas, camellia, blue hydrangeas. Bring up to pH 6/6.5 for average growing.

Apart from supplying plant foods gradually, and over a long period, compost and animal manures have other beneficial effects. The addition of such organic matter will promote good soil structure, giving an increase in the moisture-holding capability of light soils and make heavy soils more workable. Biological activity will be increased and this will help to release plant foods from the minerals in the soil. Earthworms will be encouraged, producing better aeration and drainage with their burrows, and increasing fertility with their casts which are much richer in available nutrients than is the surrounding soil.

Methods of achieving soil fertility such as composting, mulching and green manuring are described in detail in later chapters of this book, but the importance of the subject makes it worthy of further mention here. There are a number of factors which may contribute to poor soil fertility. Common examples are lack of soil air caused by waterlogging or compaction, a low level of organic matter, incorrect pH, and low population of earthworms probably caused by one or more of the other factors.

If air is driven out of the soil by compaction or by water which had filled all of the spaces between the soil particles, the conditions for growing crops will become very unfavourable. Penetration by plant roots will not be easy and the anaerobic micro-organisms, favoured by the lack of air, may produce substances which are harmful to plants. Poor soil structure in a garden may be due to the effects of heavy machinery used during house construction or to constant treading on the land during cultivation, especially if this has been done in wet weather. Methods of dealing with this problem and preventing it recurring are dealt with in the next chapter. The steps taken to

remedy compaction may also cure waterlogging. If this is not the case, it may be necessary to provide some kind of drainage system, or to turn the growing area into raised beds.

The degree of acidity or alkalinity (pH) of a soil has a marked effect on its suitability for growing particular plants. Easy-to-use pH testing kits are cheap, and come complete with a list of pH ranges suitable for various plants. A soil that is just on the acid side of neutral will be suitable for most vegetables. A number of products containing calcium can be used to raise the pH and, obviously, their addition to the soil will ensure that calcium is available as a plant food. Hydrated lime (calcium hydroxide) is a fine powder and fast acting, ground limestone (calcium carbonate) has a more gradual effect, and dolomitic limestone (a mixture of calcium and magnesium carbonate) provides a lasting supply of magnesium. Information about the amount of lime necessary to raise the pH of the soil by a given amount should be found in the leaflet supplied with the testing kit.

Calcium compounds have a further use in gardening and this is concerned with the problem of sticky clay soils. The HDRA recommends a mixture of 80% gypsum (calcium sulphate) and 20% dolomitic limestone scattered on the soil at a rate of 8oz/sq yd. The mixture can be applied at any time of the year, but usually in spring or autumn, and should be mixed with the top couple of inches of soil using a hoe. After one or two dressings used at the above rate, an annual dressing of 2oz/sq yd should be sufficient to keep the soil in a workable condition. Further improvement in the structure of a clay soil can be achieved by adding as much organic matter as possible. This can be in the form of compost, animal manure, green manure crops and seaweed meal.

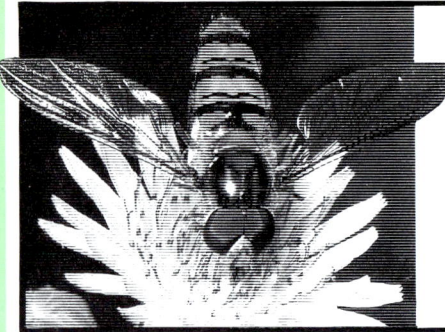

3 To Dig or Not to Dig

Most gardeners regard regular digging of their soil as a necessary part of successful vegetable growing. As there seems to be no counterpart in nature for this massive, annual soil disturbance, I think that it is worthwhile examining the reasons why it is carried out.

Reasons for Digging

- To loosen soil that has been trodden down during the growing season
- To remove large stones etc
- To break up a hard soil pan
- To enable compost and manure to be incorporated in the soil
- To remove weeds
- To remove the current crop
- To plant potatoes

Perhaps I should have included 'To provide exercise and satisfaction' in the above list because I have spoken to people who really enjoy digging. However, there are many others who are unable or unwilling to perform this rather arduous task as a matter of routine. I believe that more gardeners would take on, and persevere with, allotments if they realised that a no-dig system is feasible. The HDRA tested such a system on its trial ground with favourable results and in my own garden five years of no-digging has also been successful.

Before trying to put a no-dig system into operation in a particular situation, it is necessary to decide which of the reasons for digging are valid and what alternative methods can be used to satisfy the requirements of those that are. The amount of compaction damage caused by treading on the soil during cultivation and picking of crops will depend on a number of factors including soil type, wetness of the land at the time of treading and the amount of walking up and down that is done. One way of avoiding this problem altogether is to turn the growing area into beds and restrict treading to paths between them.

The breaking up of a hard soil pan and the removal of large stones can obviously be done by digging just once. Although it is common practice to dig in compost and manures, I have found it quite satisfactory to apply them to the surface of the soil. I sieve the compost before applying it and rely on hoeing and the action of earthworms to incorporate it into the soil. Land that has been unused for a number of years can be brought back into cultivation by digging, but this does require a considerable effort. The problem of weeds in this situation is usually dealt with either by forking them out or by turning them into the soil so that they die. Mulching is a much easier method of bringing soil back into cultivation and this is fully described in Chapter 9; the technique of growing no-dig potatoes is also covered in this chapter. Root crops such as carrots and parsnips can be removed without actually digging, but if they are particularly deep-rooted it may be necessary to loosen the soil by pushing in a fork and then levering backwards slightly.

Up to now, I have been approaching the idea of no-digging as if it were a second-best alternative for gardeners who wish to save time and energy. Although I consider this a very good reason for giving up digging, I also believe that there are a number of other advantages.

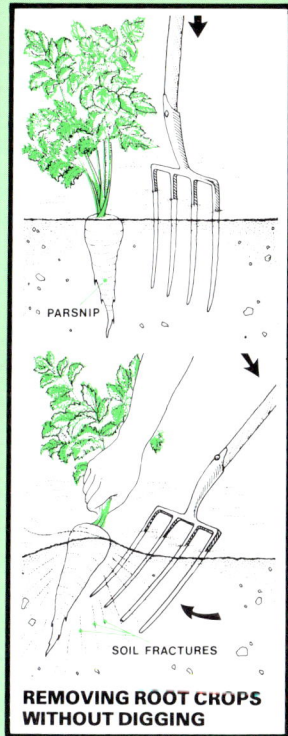

REMOVING ROOT CROPS
WITHOUT DIGGING

PARSNIP

SOIL FRACTURES

Far left:

Digging may be fun for some people . . .

Left:

. . . but 'back-breaking' for others.

Advantages of No-digging

● A considerable amount of hard work is avoided
● Subsoil will not be brought to the surface during digging operations
● The most fertile part of the soil — that is the top few inches — will not be buried below the reach of plant roots
● Similarly, compost and manure placed on the soil surface will not be put beyond the reach of plants
● The good soil structure, built by earthworms, will not be broken up by digging

As I have already mentioned, compaction of the growing area can be avoided by using a system of beds and paths. I adopted this layout some years ago in my garden and would now describe the system that I use as 'No-dig — No Tread', although I must admit this title sounds like a health warning or advertising slogan.

Advantages of Using a Bed and Path Layout

● By walking only on the paths between the beds, compaction of the growing area can be avoided
● Crops can be harvested during wet weather without damaging the soil structure
● When plants are grown in conventional rows, space may be wasted because the rows have to be far enough apart for the gardener to walk between them and carry out cultivation. On the bed system, the spacing between plants has only to be based on their requirements, and not on the gardener's
● The close spacing mentioned above means that many vegetables can be grown so they provide a complete canopy of foliage which will protect the soil surface from damage by heavy rain, and reduce the germination of weed seeds

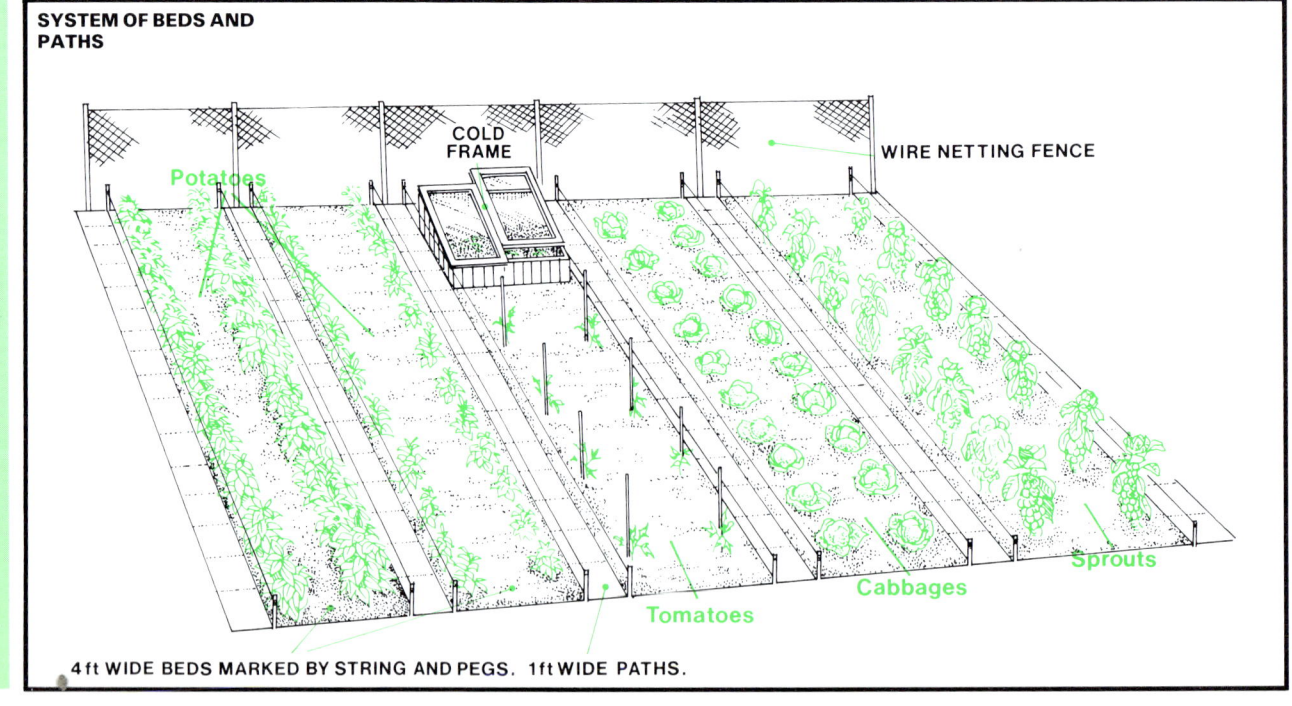

SYSTEM OF BEDS AND PATHS

COLD FRAME

WIRE NETTING FENCE

Potatoes

Tomatoes

Cabbages

Sprouts

4ft WIDE BEDS MARKED BY STRING AND PEGS. 1ft WIDE PATHS.

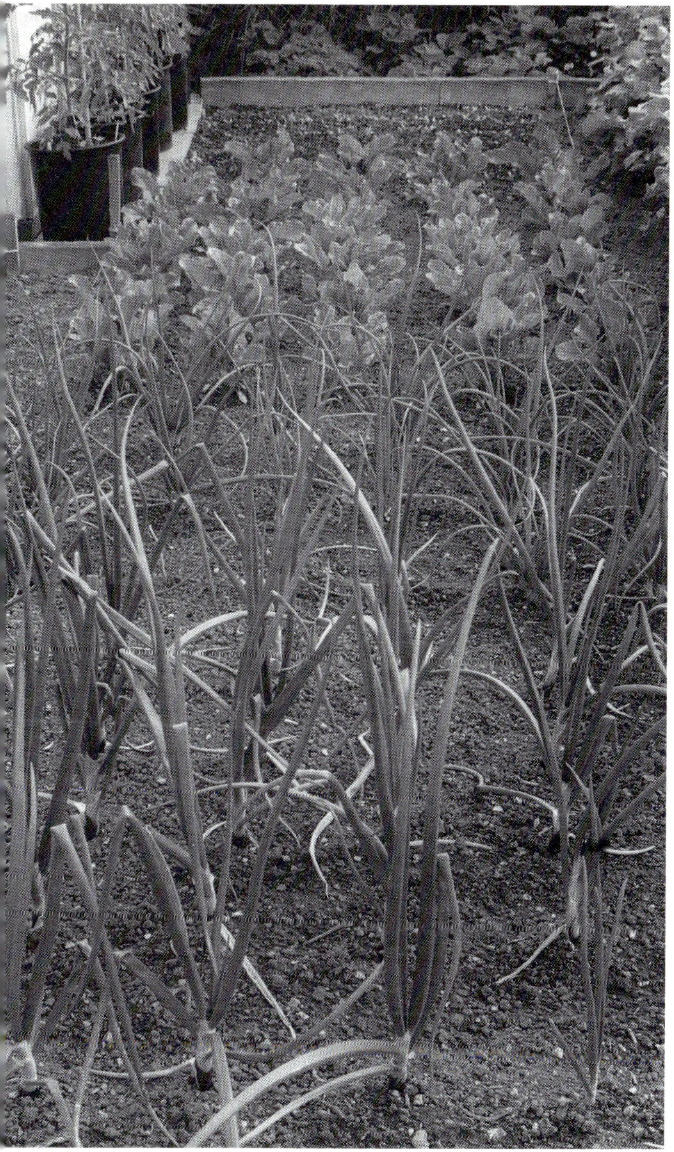

Far left:
Onions and multiple-sown beetroot growing on a 4ft-wide bed.

Left:
On a bed system, plant spacing can be closer than with conventional rows.

Below:
Weeds do not present a problem with the close spacing used for these Minicole cabbages.

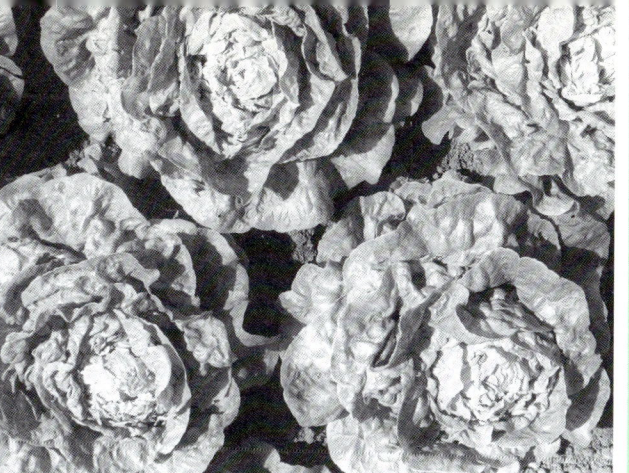

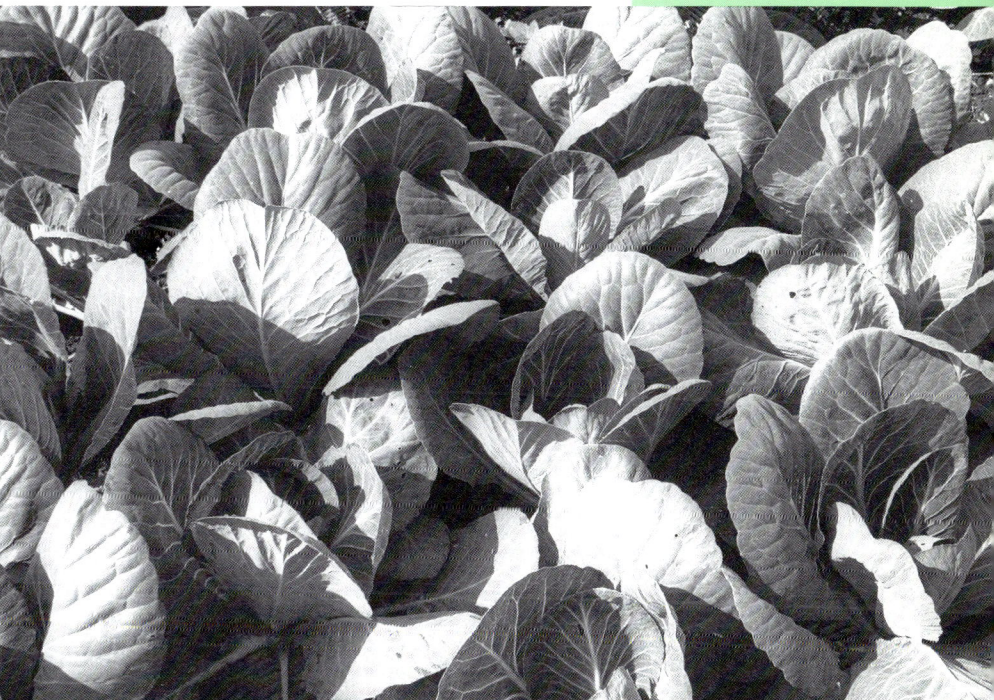

Raised Beds

Gardeners who have trouble with drainage are likely to benefit from having raised beds, and this can be achieved by building them up with soil taken from the paths. Application of compost and manure will also increase the height of the beds. Raised beds can either be shaped to give a convex surface, or some sort of retaining wall can be used and the surface kept flat. Another advantage of moving earth from the paths on to the beds is the increased depth of soil available for plants. When I set up the beds in my garden, loosening of the soil and the addition of manure raised them above the level of the paths. During subsequent cultivation I found the convex shape to be a nuisance and so, as my soil does not require extra drainage, I allowed the beds to settle and have not added extra soil.

● **Setting up the Beds**

Before any practical work is started, it is necessary to decide how wide the paths and beds are to be. The wider the beds the greater the growing area available, but this must be weighed against the ease with which the gardener can reach at least half way across the beds for the purpose of cultivation. Conversely, the paths should be as narrow as possible to avoid wasting space, but must be wide enough to allow the gardener to work comfortably. For my own requirements, I find that a bed width of 4ft with 1ft wide paths is fine.

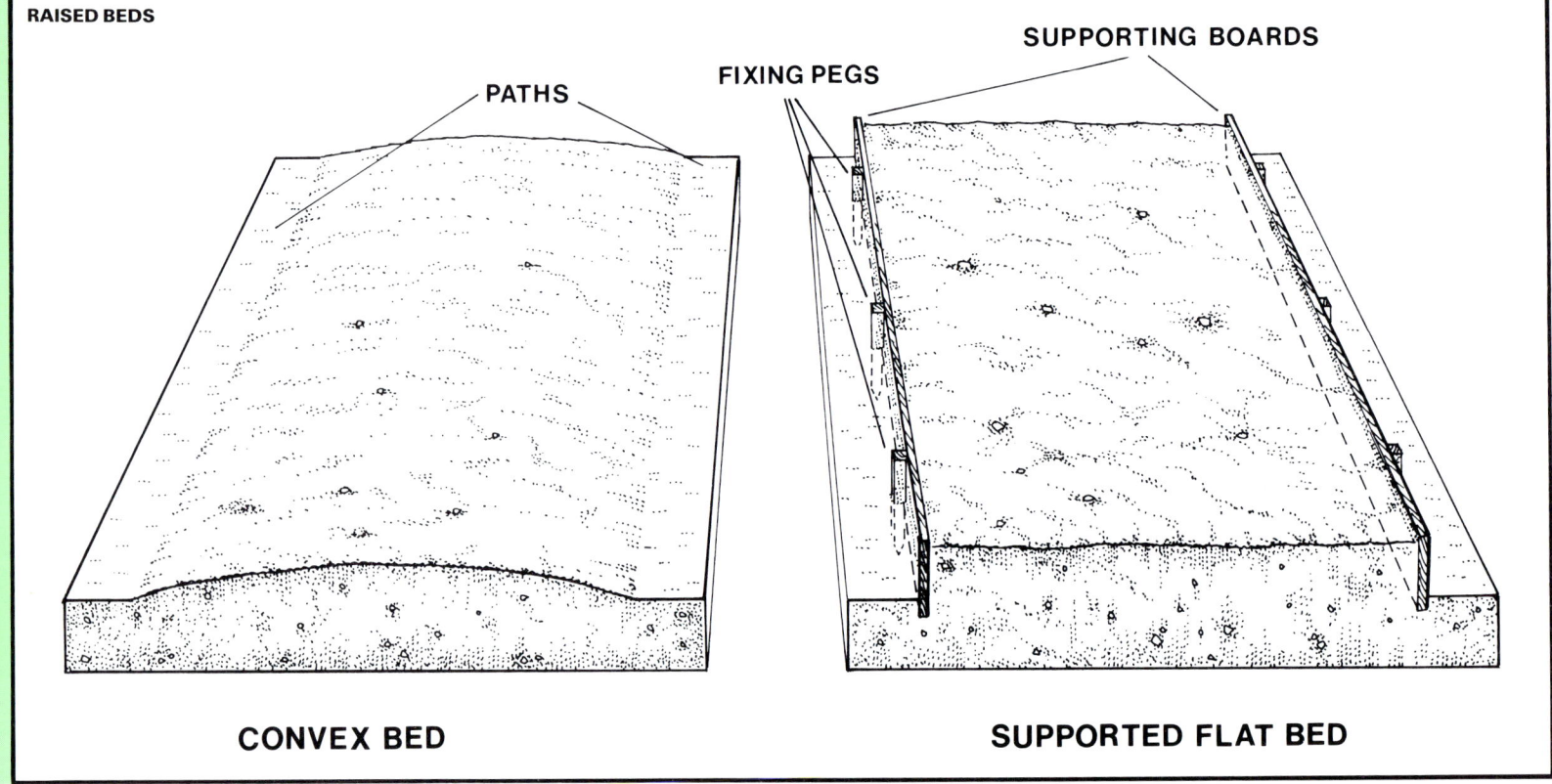

RAISED BEDS

PATHS

FIXING PEGS

SUPPORTING BOARDS

CONVEX BED

SUPPORTED FLAT BED

Far left, top:

It is necessary to be able to reach halfway across a bed so that operations such as weeding can be carried out.

Far left, bottom:

Hoeing can be done from the paths using a long-handled hoe . . .

Left:

. . . or one with a shorter handle and narrow blade if less space is available between plants.

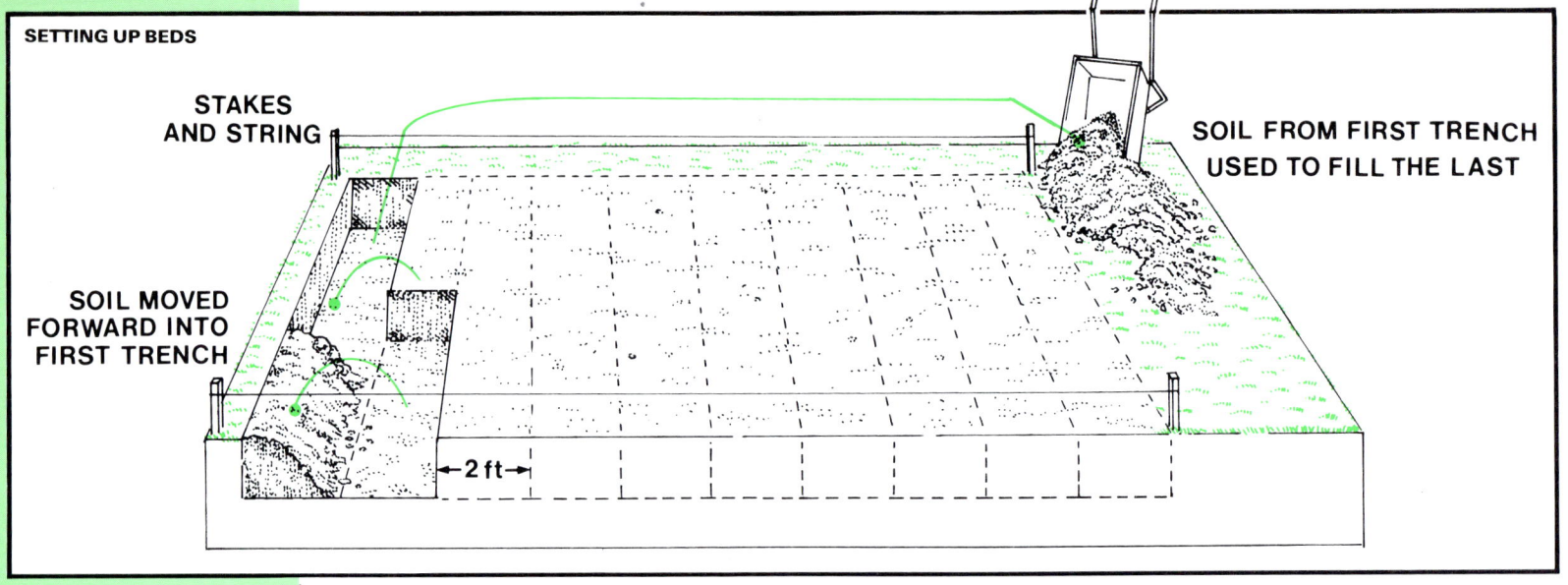

SETTING UP BEDS

STAKES
AND STRING

SOIL FROM FIRST TRENCH
USED TO FILL THE LAST

SOIL MOVED
FORWARD INTO
FIRST TRENCH

←2 ft→

● Method

1. Two measuring sticks are required, one with a length equal to the width of the bed, eg 4ft, and one with a length of 2ft. 1in × 1in timber or a garden cane can be used and one of the sticks should be marked out with the width of path required, eg 1ft, using plastic tape or a saw cut.

2. Starting at one end of the garden, mark out the first bed using wooden stakes knocked into the ground with string between them.

3. Using the shorter measuring stick, mark out a distance of 2ft from the end of the bed.

4. Slice down the perimeter of the marked-out area by pushing a spade into the ground.

5. Remove the soil from within the marked area and place it at one side of the other end of the bed. Do not dig any deeper than the depth of the topsoil.

6. Loosen the subsoil with a fork. This should be done by pushing in the fork as far as possible and then levering backwards to raise and break up the subsoil.

7. Mark out another 2ft-wide section and move the soil from it forward into the hole created by digging out the first section. Compost or manure can be incorporated into the soil at any desired depth at this stage.

8. Repeat the process until the end of the bed is reached and then use the soil removed from the first section to fill up the hole left in the last.

9. Mark out the rest of the garden into beds and paths and use the above method to prepare them for use.

The above method is the one that I used to prepare the beds in my garden about five years ago. Since then the soil has not been dug, all compost and manure being applied to the soil surface. I am unsure whether I gained any benefit from digging when setting up the beds, as the soil had been dug in previous years when I grew my vegetables more conventionally in rows. If a garden or allotment has recently been dug and is free from weeds and rubbish, I do not think that further digging is necesssary. Just mark out the beds with wooden stakes and string, then use the technique of levering backwards with a fork to loosen any soil that has been trodden down. Later in this book there is an account of how to deal with overgrown land using a mulch. After this technique has been used to kill off the weeds, it should be easier to judge whether factors such as soil compaction and the presence of large stones make digging desirable, or whether a no-dig system can be started immediately.

Left:
**Making seed drills across a
bed with a home-made tool.**

Mechanical Cultivators

There is quite a range of mechanical cultivators on the market and these machines can be used to replace hand digging as a means of breaking up the soil. The more expensive machines with powerful motors and large tines are capable of dealing with large areas of rough ground, but even a small cultivator can be useful on an average-sized allotment or garden. Although I only use hand tools in my garden, I do make use of a small mechanical cultivator on my allotment. Because I have to travel to my allotment, I spend less time there than in my garden and this, combined with the number of weed seeds blown in from surrounding vacant plots, is why I cultivate it using a different system. I have marked out the allotment into beds and paths but I do tread on the whole area occasionally while using the cultivator. The machine is not used to replace deep digging with a spade or fork, but provides a means of incorporating partly decayed mulches into the top few inches of soil. Its other function is as a kind of mechanical hoe for killing weeds on soil that is awaiting crops.

Left:
A mechanical cultivator being used on a new allotment.

Above:
Cultivator tines break up soil effectively and are easy to remove for cleaning.

4
Composing

Below:
Various types of compost containers displayed at Ryton Gardens.

In this chapter, the term 'compost' is used to describe partly decomposed plant and animal waste and does not refer to seed and potting mixtures such as John Innes Compost.

Compost plays a vital role in organic gardening and offers the following advantages:

● **Smoking Bonfires can be Avoided**
During the summer, it seems to need only a sunny day to start some gardeners scouring their land for the greenest, wettest material with which to make a bonfire. Not only does this create toxic smoke, but it also deprives the soil of valuable organic matter. Some materials such as thick branches may have to be burnt, but bonfires should be the exception, not the rule.

● **Recycling of Nutrients**
The minerals gathered by a plant during its life can be returned to the soil by using compost. The variety of waste plant material usually put on a heap should ensure that these plant foods are in well balanced proportions and, as compost breaks down slowly in the soil, they will be available over a long period.

● **Improvement of Soil Structure**
Better soil structure will provide air spaces for plant roots and prevent waterlogging.

● **Improved Moisture and Nutrient-Holding Capability**
The water-holding capacity of light soils can be considerably improved by the addition of compost. Organic matter has the ability to reduce the amount of plant foods washed out of the soil by rain.

● **Enhanced Biological Activity**
The use of compost will produce a large increase in the number of beneficial soil micro-organisms, earthworms and predatory insects.

Composting Display

Below right:
TYPICAL COMPOSTING MATERIALS: green manures, straw, fruit tree prunings, privet, hay, carrot tops, weeds, lettuce leaves and cabbage leaves.

Given time and suitable conditions, all animal and vegetable wastes will decay and release their plant foods. Almost all such material can therefore be composted, but it is better to exclude some materials because of practical reasons or because they are contaminated.

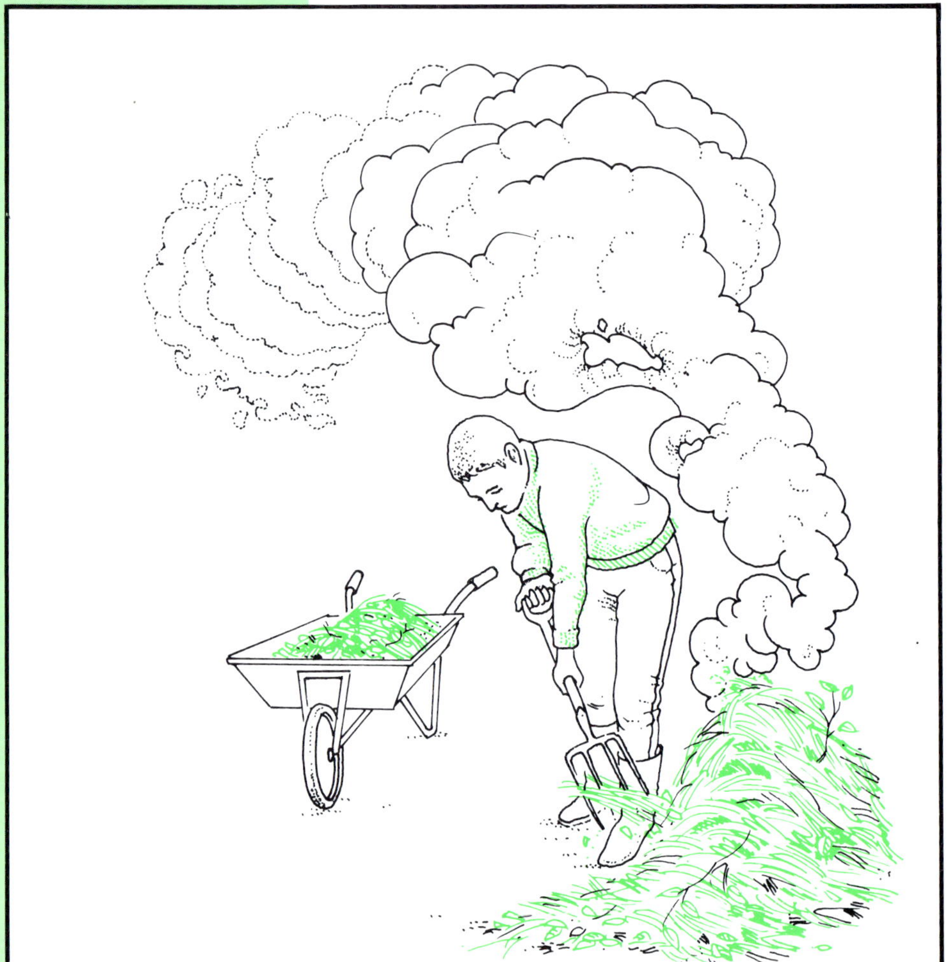

SMOKING BONFIRE

Materials Suitable for Composting

● Soft, Wet Materials

Grass mowings, tea leaves, weeds, fruit, vegetable peelings, outer leaves of brassicas, carrot tops, rhubarb leaves and potato haulm.

● Stemmy Materials Containing Less Moisture

Hedge clippings, summer prunings of fruit trees, straw, sweet corn stems and leaves, sunflower stems and hay.

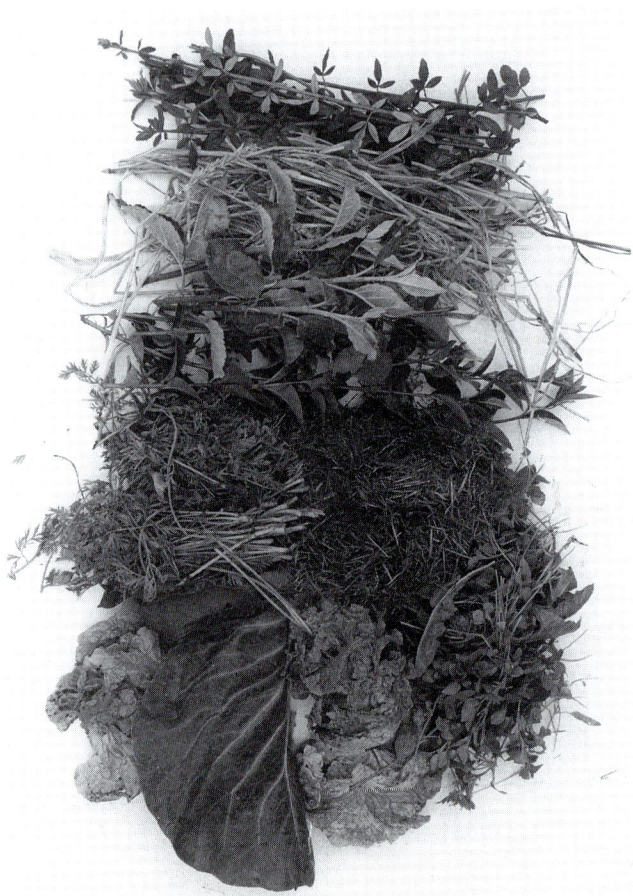

Unsuitable Materials

Plastic, metal, brassica plants suffering from clubroot, thick branches, prunings from roses, pyracanthas etc which have thorns that can make the removal of finished compost hazardous, vacuum cleaner dust and paper on which coloured inks have been used.

Weeds

Many gardening writers recommend that perennial weeds and weeds that have seeded should be destroyed by burning. I have not taken this advice and instead I recycle my weeds through the compost heap so that I do not waste valuable organic matter or produce toxic bonfire smoke. A number of factors influence whether or not live weed seeds and roots appear in finished compost.

● **Heat**
The chance of killing roots and seeds will be maximised by placing the weeds in the centre of the heap and by making sure that it reaches a high temperature. A heap built from fresh animal manure and straw is an ideal place in which to kill weeds.

● **Exclusion of Light**
A lightproof compost container will prevent the manufacture of food by perennial weeds and will eventually kill them. The large amount of food stored in the roots of some weeds means that they may take a considerable length of time to die. Bindweed and couch grass should not be allowed to grow close to maturing compost because their roots may grow sideways into the heap.

● **Physical Damage**
Roots from weeds such as dandelions and docks will die more quickly if they are cut up or smashed before composting.

● **Desiccation**
Drying in the sun is a method of killing or weakening weeds before putting them on the compost heap.

Whenever possible, the obvious and best way of preventing weed seeds appearing in finished compost is to pull up or hoe the weeds before they have a chance to set seed. If problems are experienced with perennial weed roots surviving normal composting, they can be kept separate from the rest of the heap and killed by immersion in water. As mentioned in another part of this book, I once had two large buckets full of bindweed roots which I had removed from the soil together with a privet hedge. I put the bindweed in a water butt which I then topped up to half full with water. The roots were kept below the surface of the water with a couple of bricks, and were then left to die. The process was successful in killing the roots and producing liquid manure from them, but did produce an unpleasant smell when the water butt was emptied. I have not experimented further with this technique because I do not normally have a problem killing perennial weeds, but I do think it would be useful to some gardeners if the smell could be reduced. Perhaps increasing the volume of water for a given amount of weeds would help.

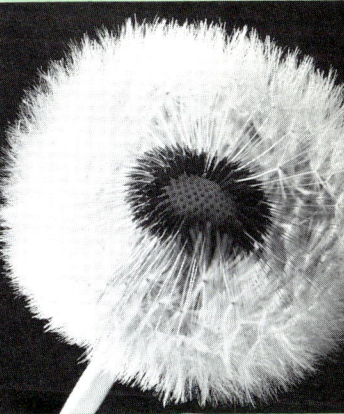

Left:
Pyracantha flowers and berries are very attractive, but the thorns can give a painful injection if the prunings are put in a compost heap.

Above:
It is unwise to allow weeds such as dandelions to form seeds.

Compost Activators

There are a number of substances that can be added to a compost heap to promote decomposition. With the exception of animal manure, I have found the effectiveness of these activators to be difficult to assess because other factors can vary so much.

● Animal Manure

If a reasonable supply of animal manure can be obtained and added to a heap, there should be no difficulty in getting the compost to heat up and decompose satisfactorily. Stable manure (horse manure and straw) is excellent for this purpose and should be used fresh.

● Seaweed Meal

This is used to provide a food supply for bacteria so that these organisms can multiply rapidly. Only a light 'dusting' is required on each layer of composting material as the heap is built up.

● Bacterial Preparations

These are cultures of micro-organisms which have been chosen because of their ability to convert vegetable waste into compost.

● Herbal Activator

This product, known as QR (Quick Return) Compost Activator, was invented by the late Maye E. Bruce and is mixed with water before use.

● Re-using Old Compost

Any coarse material that does not decompose sufficiently during one composting process can be re-used in a new heap where it will decay further and also provide a supply of bacteria and fungi. Soil contains micro-organisms that will break down composting material and these will enter the heap if it is built directly on the ground.

Compost Containers

A compost container should have the following features:

● Sufficient Size

This will depend on the amount of composting material available.

● Drainage

It is likely that at some time vegetable waste containing an excessive amount of water will be put in the container and this must be allowed to drain away.

● A Lid to Keep Out Rain

● Heat Insulation

Retaining the considerable amount of heat generated by a good

CONICAL COMPOST BIN

compost heap will ensure speedy decomposition and help to destroy weed seeds and perennial weeds.

● Easy Access to Finished Compost
Mature compost is a rather heavy material and so a container design that allows it to be removed easily will save a lot of hard work.

● Resistance to Rotting
Some materials used in the construction of compost containers are attacked by the micro-organisms present in the heap. The life expectancy of a particular material should therefore be taken into account when considering it for this purpose.

● Reasonable Price
If second-hand materials can be obtained locally, it is likely that the cost of making a container will be less than the price of a ready-made bin.

Many people, including some manufacturers, believe that compost containers require *Ventilation Holes*. In my opinion, the disadvantage of these holes, especially with small containers, is that they have a cooling effect. The advantage gained by having insulation around a heap can easily be lost by letting heat escape in this way. Sufficient air should be present in the layers of vegetable waste built up in a container for it to heat up, provided that it is not packed in too tightly. Once the initial heat has died down, forking the material out of the container and mixing it as it is returned will provide a fresh supply of air. The compost should heat up again and can be left to mature until ready for use.

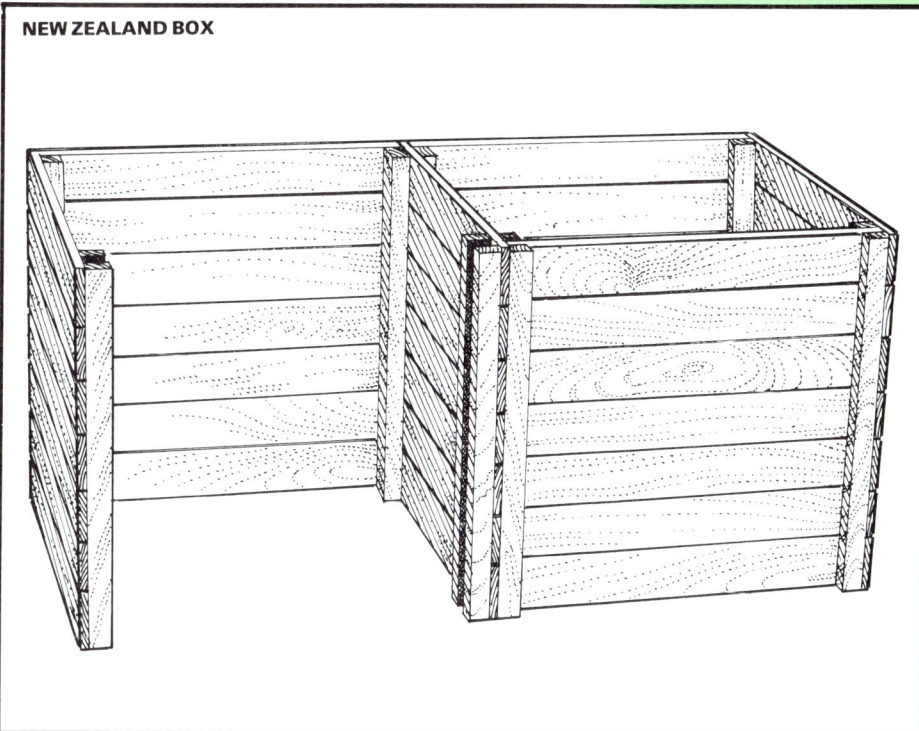

NEW ZEALAND BOX

Examples of Compost Containers

● New Zealand Box
This two-compartment container has removable front boards to allow easy access to mature compost, and was named after its country of origin. The advantage of having the box split into two sections is that compost can be left to mature in one side, while fresh material is being built up in the other. The standard-sized box is composed of two cubes measuring 3ft in each direction, but the size can be chosen to accommodate the amount of composting material available. Constructing a decent-sized New Zealand Box from new timber would be a rather expensive proposition, but the cost can be cut considerably by using second-hand floorboards. The thickness of timber used will obviously determine the amount of insulation provided by the box.

Construction of a New Zealand Box is straightforward and consists of nailing wooden planks to upright posts. Burying the ends of these posts in the ground will help to prevent the sides of the box being forced outwards by the weight of composting material.

The life of the box will be increased if the timber is soaked in preservative before construction.

● Conical Plastic Bin
This is a lightweight, bottomless container that can be used on a spare part of the garden to make compost. The removable lid allows material to be placed in the container, and access to the contents is simply a matter of lifting off the bin.

● Insulated Compost Box
The insulated compost box is made by sandwiching polystyrene foam between two sheets of *oil tempered* hardboard. Economic use of standard-sized hardboard dictates the box sizes —

2ft×2ft×2ft OR 3ft×2ft 6in×2ft 6in. The smaller size is useful for making worm compost and the larger size for garden compost.

Construction is straightforward and consists of making four equal-sized sides, joining three together, and hinging the fourth as a door. I used three layers of polystyrene ceiling tiles, a total thickness of about ¾in, to insulate my compost box, but the 1in-thick polystyrene slabs sold by builder's merchants would be an alternative. Obviously, the thickness of the framing timber must match the total thickness of the insulation. Use 2in nails as steel dowels to join the corners of the framing, pilot holes being used to prevent splitting of the timber. During the construction of my box I cut all of the framing to size and then soaked it in wood preservative. The timber was allowed to dry thoroughly, to prevent the solvent attacking the polystyrene, and then was fixed to the rough side of the hardboard with the type of nails

and adhesive used for roofing felt. This method of fixing was chosen because I already had the materials mentioned and has proved to be satisfactory. Waterproof adhesive and smaller nails might be a better idea, preservative only being applied to timber not being glued in this case.

Cut the hardboard to the sizes shown on the appropriate plan and then fix the framing on to each of four pieces using either of the above methods. The spaces formed by the framing can then be filled with the polystyrene which can be cut to size using a straightedge and Stanley knife. Next fix on the other sheets of hardboard and put in the corner dowels mentioned above. Planing the edges flush and treating them with preservative will complete the sides. Join three of the slabs together with large screws and fix on the door using hinges which should be painted prior to fixing and regularly oiled to prevent rust. Fillets

---

INSULATED COMPOST BOX

CUTTING PLAN (FROM TWO 8'x 4' HARDBOARD SHEETS) FOR THE 3'x 2'6" BOX.
FOR A 2'x 2' BOX, CUT ONE 8'x4' SHEET INTO EIGHT PIECES 2'x 2'

Wood blocks for steel bolts

COMPOSTING IN A POLYTHENE BAG

WEEDS

of wood may be fixed in the back corners of the box to keep it square. An inexpensive method of keeping the door closed and located is shown in the diagram. Wooden blocks are fixed to the side and to the door of the box and are then drilled to accept nuts and bolts.

A suggested lid is shown in the diagram, but any method of keeping rain out will do. Insulation at the top of the box can be provided by using bubble polythene, a material often discarded after being used for packaging. A wooden platform, supported on insulating material, can be used to reduce heat loss into the soil. Drainage holes must be drilled in the platform and the insulation can be bubble polythene, broken polystyrene foam, straw etc.

● **Black Polythene Bag**
Gardeners who only have a very small amount of composting material may find that black polythene bags will serve as acceptable containers. A few drainage holes should be made in the bottoms of the bags and, when full, they can be stored out of sight while the contents mature. This is a good method of dealing with perennial weeds, and weeds that have a lot of soil on their roots.

Building a Compost Heap

The following principles apply when building compost heaps in most types of container.

The excessive amount of liquid often produced during composting can cause waterlogging of the lower layers if drainage is not provided. Starting a heap with a fairly thick layer of coarse material such as hedge trimmings will allow this liquid to drain away. Some people recommend that bricks should be used to provide air channels at the base of the heap for the purpose of ventilation, but I have not found this to be necessary. As previously mentioned, I find that the air trapped by composting material when it is stacked, plus that which is introduced by turning, is sufficient.

Once the porous layer is in place, building of the heap can be continued with whatever vegetable waste is available. It is advisable to mix soft, wet materials with those that are harder and drier because the two types complement each other. For example, lawn mowings will heat up very quickly but will soon form a soggy, anaerobic mass unless mixed with drier material. On the other hand, sweet corn stems and leaves are rather dry for composting on their own, and therefore benefit from being mixed with something wetter. If a proprietary activator has been chosen, it should be used as directed. Seaweed meal or animal manure should be used by applying them to each 6-9in layer of vegetable waste. Opinions differ as to whether or not it is necessary to use lime in a compost heap. The purpose of adding this substance is to neutralise the acids that are formed during decomposition, especially in heaps that are short of air. If it is decided to use lime, it should be scattered lightly on to the layers of vegetable waste as the heap is built, but should not come into contact with animal manure.

When the composting material reaches the top of the container, it should be left for a while. This is to allow the initial heat to build up in the compost, and then die away. After a few weeks, when the compost has cooled, it should be removed from the container and then forked back in again. This stage provides a good opportunity to break up any large lumps of compost, and to ensure that it is well mixed. The fresh supply of air will cause the compost to re-heat and decompose further. The total amount of time taken to turn vegetable waste into finished compost varies a great deal, and is influenced by factors such as ambient temperature, type of composting material used and size of heap. As a rough guide, I would say that composting should be complete after a period of between six weeks and six months.

I apologise for making composting appear so complicated, but I have included a fair amount of information so that

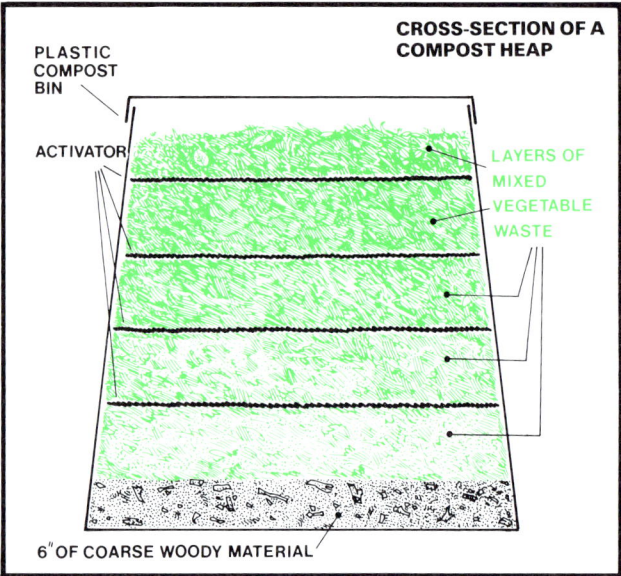

PLASTIC COMPOST BIN

ACTIVATOR

CROSS-SECTION OF A COMPOST HEAP

LAYERS OF MIXED VEGETABLE WASTE

6" OF COARSE WOODY MATERIAL

Mature Compost

The term 'maturing' does not have exactly the same meaning when applied to compost as it does when applied to people. The obvious difference is that human beings should mature as they grow up, whereas compost tends to sink down while maturing. During the initial stage of decomposition, when a great deal of heat is produced, composting material undergoes rapid changes that can easily be seen. Quite a large reduction in volume may take place as plant tissues break down, and there will be a marked change in the colour of the composting material. Eventually, the compost will reach a stage where it has cooled down and will not re-heat, even if more air is introduced. Further decomposition then becomes very slow. The exact time at which compost becomes mature enough to use depends on its intended use and the gardener's preference. As a guide, I would say that compost is sufficiently mature when the original material has broken down beyond recognition, and the final product has only a faint, earthy smell.

individual gardeners can make the best use of the construction materials and composting materials available to them.

The following step-by-step guide is given as an example and can be modified to suit a gardener's raw materials and preferences.

1. Place a 6in layer of coarse, woody material in the bottom of the container.
2. Build up a 6-9in layer of vegetable waste. If possible, mix wet and dry, fine and coarse materials. Thick stemmed vegetables such as brassicas should have their stems smashed before they are used.
3. Dust the surface of the heap with seaweed meal.
4. Add more layers and seaweed meal until the top of the container is reached.
5. Cover with old carpet or bubble polythene to keep in the heat.
6. Allow the heap to heat up and then cool.
7. Remove the contents from the container, mix with a fork, and then re-stack the heap.
8. After re-heating, the compost should be left to mature before using. If the container is required because more fresh material has become available, the compost can be removed and stored under black polythene to finish maturing.

Right:
Mature compost.

Far right:
Applying compost to the surface of the soil.

Faults With Compost

There are two main reasons why a compost heap may have been unsuccessful.

● Too Wet

If the proportion of composting material containing a lot of water is too high, the heap will become waterlogged and devoid of air. Anaerobic decomposition will then take place, producing unpleasant smells and a slimy end product. In this case the material should be removed from the compost container, partially dried in the sun (if possible), and then mixed with something drier such as hay before being re-stacked.

● Too Dry

It is easy to tell if compost is too dry because the original material will remain almost unchanged. If only small pockets of the heap are found to be too dry, mixing may be sufficient to solve the problem. Overall dryness can be cured by watering with a hose or mixing in lawn mowings, and then re-making the heap.

Using Compost

For most gardeners, the biggest problem with compost is making it in sufficient quantity, and so careful consideration should be given to the ways in which it can be used most effectively.

● In Planting Holes

This is a very economical method of using a small amount of compost and ensuring that it is 'explored' by plant roots. Make a larger than normal planting hole, place enough compost in the hole to raise the plant to the correct height, and then fill in with a mixture of soil and compost.

● In a Trench

The moisture-holding capability of compost can be exploited by burying it in a trench for crops such as runner beans.

● Incorporated During Digging

This can be achieved by spreading compost on the ground and then mixing it with the soil as this is turned over.

● As a Top Dressing

With no-dig systems, compost must obviously be applied to the surface of the soil. It can then be either left as a mulch or mixed with the surface layer of soil using a hoe or rake.

USING COMPOST

SOIL/COMPOST MIX

COMPOST

IN A HOLE

COMPOST

IN A TRENCH

SOIL/COMPOST MIX

DUG INTO SOIL

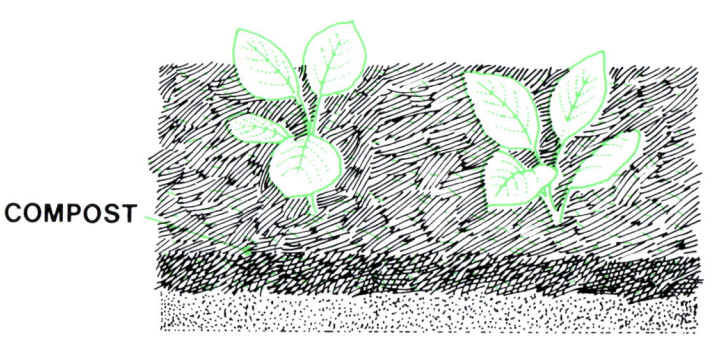

COMPOST

AS A TOP DRESSING

Leafmould

If leaves that have fallen from trees in the autumn are available in quantity, it is better not to include them in a normal compost heap. A simple wire netting cage will keep the leaves tidy and contained while they decay. Leaves from different trees vary in their rates of decay but it would be reasonable to expect leafmould to be ready for use after two years. Mixing lawn mowings with leaves is one way of speeding up this process.

The value of leafmould lies in its lasting supply of organic matter rather than its poor supply of plant foods. It can be used in a similar way to peat, ie as a mulch, incorporated in the topsoil and used in potting mixtures.

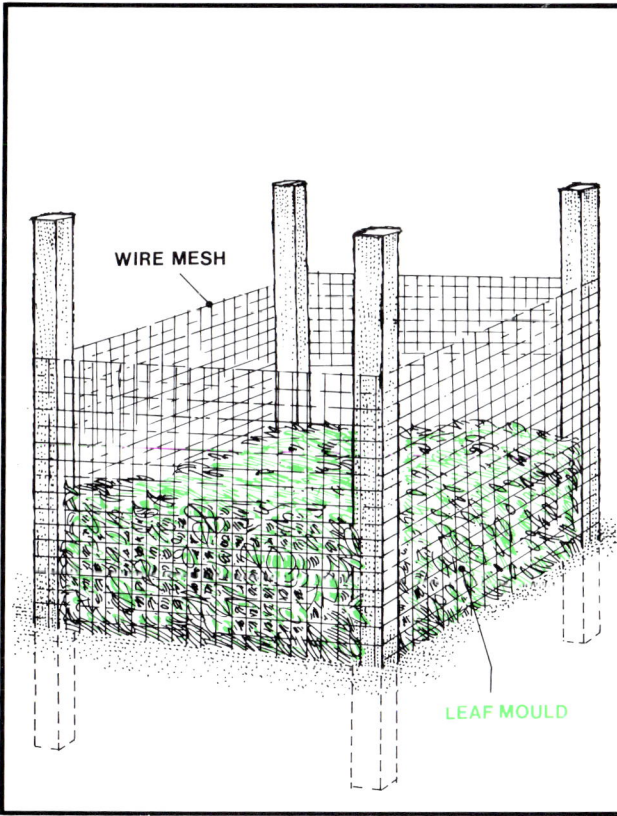

WIRE MESH

LEAF MOULD

Compost Shredders

I have separated the description and use of compost shredders from the rest of the chapter because I would not like to give the impression that these machines are essential if good compost is to be made. Shredders are available in various sizes and use either petrol or electricity as a power source. Electric motors are quieter and easier to start than petrol motors but the latter may be used in places where there is no electricity supply. The following comments are based on my experience of using the machine featured in the photographs, but I would imagine that the general principles apply to other shredders on the market.

Relatively high price, running costs and the need for storage space under cover mean that compost shredders must provide tangible benefits if their purchase is to be justified. Apart from the size of a person's bank account, I would say that the main factor which should influence the decision on whether or not to buy a shredder is the amount of tough, woody material available for composting. Soft, sappy vegetable waste does not need shredding before being composted, in fact it would tend to clog up the machine anyway. If such material is to be shredded, some of the moisture should first be removed by wilting it in the sun. Hedge trimmings, fruit tree prunings, raspberry canes, brussels sprouts stems and other similar material that is normally difficult to compost is ideal for putting through a shredder. Such material will take up far less room in a compost box after being shredded, and its damaged surfaces will quickly be attacked by bacteria and fungi.

It took me a while to develop an effective method of using my shredder, and anyone purchasing their own machine may find the following hints helpful.

1. Collect all material to be shredded before starting the machine.
2. Keep stones out of the shredder as far as possible to avoid blunting the blades.
3. The machine will not clog so easily if vegetable waste containing a relatively high level of moisture is mixed with drier material as it is being fed in.
4. Feed woody material such as buddleia prunings and raspberry canes into the side tube of the shredder whenever possible.

Since I have been shredding my compost material, I have found that even quite small amounts heat up very well. This is helped by the use of an insulated box, described earlier in the chapter, and the fact that I am careful to use a mixture of materials.

Above:
Brussels sprouts stems ready for shredding.

Far right:
Shredder in action.

Right:
Bowl of shredded material.

Left:
Cleaning of the shredder blades is easy once the upper section is removed.

Right:
The combination of shredded compost material and an insulated bin should produce high temperatures.

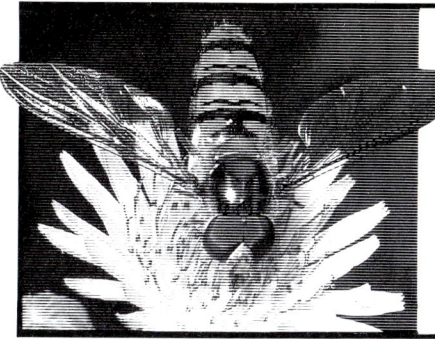

5 Worm Composting

Below:
Manure worms.

Brandlings (manure worms) have long been used as bait by fishermen. Recently, however, the by-product of breeding these worms, ie worm casts, has been recognised as a valuable source of plant foods and organic matter. Although it is possible to buy worm compost, most gardeners should find it easy to produce an adequate supply of their own.

Materials Suitable for Worm Composting

Worm compost can be used to replace ordinary compost or manure in situations where these materials would normally be employed, but I think that the best use of a limited supply is as a component of potting mixtures. This means that weed seeds and woody material that will not break down easily should be excluded when making worm compost, especially as the high temperatures achieved in normal compost heaps do not occur. Kitchen waste is an ideal raw material for worm composting. Provided that the worm bin is of a type that cannot be entered by rodents, cooked food may be used in addition to uncooked items such as carrot tops, outer leaves of cabbages and fruit skins.

Cutting up the composting material will accelerate decomposition because it gives the worms and micro-organisms a greater surface area on which to work. There is a limit to what can be gained in this direction however, because cutting up too finely allows compaction and exclusion of air. I once tried making worm compost out of kitchen waste that had been put through a compost shredder. The result was a soggy, anaerobic mess which gave off a foul smell.

The use of a fibrous material such as peat or leafmould has a couple of advantages in worm composting. Firstly, a more open texture can be obtained, admitting air and reducing stickiness.

Secondly, dry peat or leafmould can be used to absorb excess moisture and so reduce unpleasant odours. As peat is generally regarded as a useful constituent of potting mixtures, I think that its cost is justified if the worm compost is to be used for this purpose. Torn-up newspaper can be used to replace or supplement peat and does have the advantage of nil cost.

As decomposition proceeds, the contents of a worm bin can become rather sour, especially if there is a lack of air. The conditions may be made less acid, and therefore more favourable to worms, by the use of calcified seaweed or ground limestone.

Containers

Various types of container can be used for worm composting, but a number of factors should be considered before a choice is made. As with normal composting, the construction material needs to have good resistance to decay, otherwise the life of the container will be very short. Worm compost tends to be wetter and therefore heavier than normal compost, and so it is unwise to build it up too high in case compaction of the lower layers occurs. For this reason, worm boxes should not be as deep as the compost containers described in the previous chapter.

Right:
MATERIALS FOR WORM COMPOSTING: vegetable waste, worms, calcified seaweed and sedge peat.

Worms need protection against frost and this can be provided by insulating the container or keeping it in a greenhouse during the winter. It is almost certain that surplus liquid will be produced when worm compost is made from kitchen waste. This liquid manure can be allowed to drain on to the soil or it can be caught in a collection chamber, diluted and fed to plants.

Initial Supply of Worms

It is important to use the correct species of worm when setting up a bin for the first time. The type required (brandlings) can be identified by the red and yellow bands which circle their bodies. It should be possible to obtain an initial supply of these worms from a compost or manure heap, but they can also be bought in the form of worm capsules. These capsules or eggs should produce about four worms each and can be sent through the post. Once a thriving colony of worms has been established in one bin, there is obviously no problem in obtaining a supply to start the next.

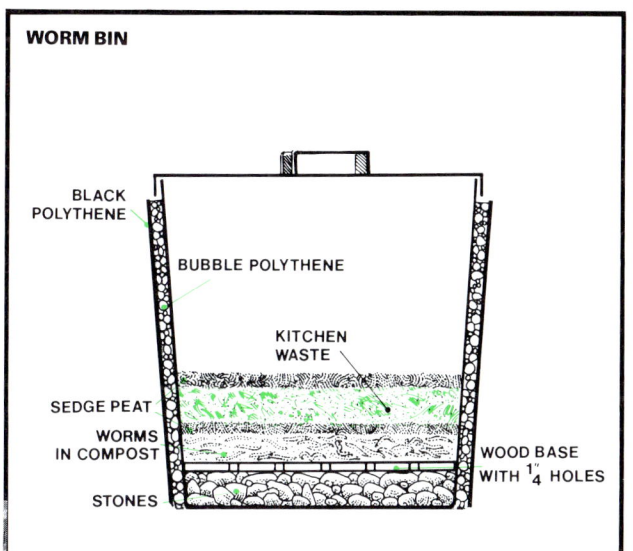

WORM BIN

BLACK POLYTHENE

BUBBLE POLYTHENE

KITCHEN WASTE

SEDGE PEAT

WORMS IN COMPOST

WOOD BASE WITH $\frac{1}{4}''$ HOLES

STONES

Worm Composting in a Plastic Dustbin

Although I have modified the technique slightly, I got the original idea for this method from Jack Temple.

When buying a dustbin, it is best to choose one that is sturdy enough not to split under the weight of worm compost, is short and wide rather than tall and narrow, and has a lid that can be fixed on securely. The bin should be prepared for use in the following manner:

1. Fill the bin to a depth of 2in with large stones. The spaces between the stones create a sump in the bottom of the bin into which liquid manure can drain.
2. Measure the diameter of the bin at the top of the stones and cut out a wooden platform of that size.
3. Drill about 20 ¼in drainage holes in the platform at roughly equal spacing.
4. With the bins that I use, the loose fitting nature of the lids, and the fact that I raise them to turn the worms, provides sufficient ventilation. If more ventilation is required, holes can be drilled around the top of the dustbin.
5. Wrapping bubble polythene around the bin will provide insulation, and a layer of black polythene on top of this will produce a neat finish.

Left:
Worm capsules.

Right:
Large stones have been placed in the bottom of the dustbin . . .

Below right:
. . . and a wooden platform has been added (this one could do with some more drainage holes).

Siting the bin near the house avoids a long walk with kitchen waste and it should be remembered that some protection from cold winds is needed during the winter.

● **Method**

1. Place some rotted compost or manure containing worms in the bin and cover with 1in of sedge peat. If compost or manure is not available, use a thicker layer of peat and a supply of worms from one of the sources mentioned above.

2. Add a 3in layer of vegetable waste.

3. Sprinkle on a small amount of calcified seaweed or ground limestone and enough sedge peat to give a layer about ½in thick. It will take the worms some time to colonise the fresh material, and no more should be added until this happens.

4. When the worms can be seen in the new material another layer may be added, complete with calcified seaweed and peat. As each layer begins to rot down, turn the contents of the bin with a fork to introduce air.

5. When the desired height of material has been reached in the bin, the worms will take about six weeks to thoroughly break down the mixture. During this time an occasional mixing with a fork should be given.

6. At the end of the maturing period, the worms will tend to congregate at the bottom of the compost (when this method of worm composting is used). This means that the top layers of worm compost can be removed virtually worm-free, and the bottom layer, complete with its worms, can be used to start a new bin.

The existence of a maturing period means that a second bin is required if worm composting is to be a continuous process. The worms will become much less active during the winter, but should survive if they do not freeze.

Worm Composting in an Insulated Box

Some time ago I made an insulated worm composting box for the HDRA. The dimensions were 2ft × 2ft × 2ft and the construction is described in Chapter 4. Pauline Pears has tested the box for several years with successful results, but using a somewhat different method to the one described above.

Instead of building up complete layers, fresh material is placed on only about half the contents of the box at a time. This leaves a cool place for the worms to live if the fresh waste gets

Left:
As an experiment, layers of vegetable waste and sedge peat have been built up in a narrow glass tank. Manure worms have also been introduced.

Below left:
After three weeks, considerable decomposition has taken place and the worms are active throughout the mixture.

too hot. No mixing with a fork is carried out and the worms move up as new layers are added. When the box is full, the top, partly decayed layer is removed complete with worms, to provide access to the fully processed compost. It is possible for the contents of the box to become too dry during the summer because it does not have a chamber for collecting liquid. If this problem does occur, water the worm compost and then cover it with wet newspaper. According to Pauline, this method of worm composting does not produce the offensive smells that are sometimes given off when other methods are used.

Storing Worm Compost

Mature worm compost may be applied to the soil straight from the bin as an alternative to normal compost. Most of mine is used for potting mixtures however, and therefore has to be stored. I always spread out the worm compost below the bench in the greenhouse, to evaporate some of the moisture, before storing it in a plastic dustbin. Drying the material in this way prevents the lower layers becoming waterlogged during storage, and makes sieving much easier.

Right:
Insulated worm compost box.

6
Organic Manures and Fertilisers

In this book I have used the term 'Manure' to describe the waste products excreted by animals. Manures generally contain considerable amounts of organic matter as well as plant foods, especially if they are composted with straw before being applied to the soil. Fertilisers, on the other hand, provide a more concentrated supply of nutrients but may contain little or no organic matter.

Manures

Most gardeners do not keep livestock and so, if manure is to be used on their soil, it must be brought in from outside. It is unlikely that a supply will be obtainable from organic farming because in this system nutrients are recycled by spreading manure on the land. Animal wastes are not so highly regarded in conventional farming however, and supplies are therefore more likely to be available from this source. Unfortunately, such manure will be subject to chemical contamination. Antibiotics and hormones fed to livestock will appear in manure, and straw is likely to contain residues of the chemicals used in cereal production. Experiments in Switzerland and Germany have shown that at least some of these chemicals can be broken down by composting. To achieve this aim, the composting process should be as long and hot as possible.

● Bagged Animal Manures

Increasing interest in organic gardening has led to the appearance of various manure-based products. These are supplied in a convenient, ready-to-use form and can be obtained from most garden centres. Having never used any of these products myself, I can only advise anyone contemplating their use to make sure that the manufacturers have been given the Soil Association Symbol.

● Horse Manure

It should be possible to obtain this very useful manure from a local riding stable. Horses are usually bedded on straw or wood shavings and these materials become mixed with urine and droppings while in use. The resulting stable manure rapidly piles up and is often given away free to any gardener wishing to

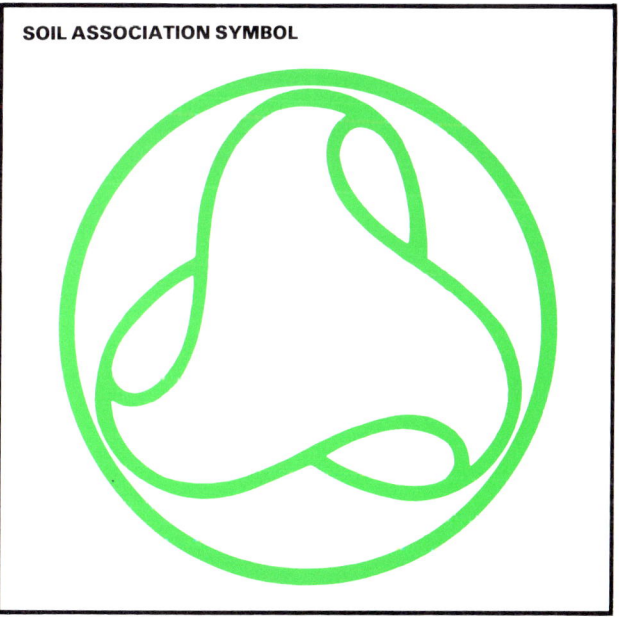

SOIL ASSOCIATION SYMBOL

collect it. As this material can provide such a valuable input to a garden, I would suggest offering at least a token payment to the owner of the establishment for each load collected. Although I prefer to use stable manure based on straw, it is also possible to use a mixture containing woodchips. There is a danger of robbing the soil of nitrogen if insufficiently decomposed woodchips are dug in, but this should not be a problem if they are mixed with sufficient manure and then well rotted before being used. The proportions of manure and woodchips will obviously depend on how frequently the stables are cleaned out, and this in turn will depend on the owners of the horses. All that a gardener can do in this respect is try to find a stable where the bedding is not changed too frequently. Collecting extra droppings and adding them to the mixture will help to some extent, but extra urine is what is really needed.

Although it means transporting a larger volume of material, I prefer to collect my stable manure fresh rather than rotted down. This gives me full control over the whole composting process and I can therefore make the best use of the heat produced. I have found a small trailer to be very useful for transporting fresh horse manure because the fumes given off by this material make it less than ideal for carrying in a car.

The container that I use for composting the manure is the same shape as the New Zealand box described in Chapter 4. This box is constructed from home-made concrete screen blocks however, with slotted concrete posts to take the front boards. The large amount of heat produced by decomposing manure makes the container's lack of insulation unimportant. I start by lining the box with black polythene and then tip in the bags of manure. Unless the manure has been subjected to heavy rain prior to collection, I find it necessary to add a certain amount of water as I build the heap. This must not be overdone however, or the result will be anaerobic decomposition and a sticky, bad-smelling end product. When all the manure has been stacked in the container, I cover it with a sheet of black polythene. After a few weeks, when the heat has built up and then subsided, I remove the contents of the container with a fork. The manure is then returned to the box, making sure that any unrotted material is placed in the centre of the heap. The fresh supply of air introduced in this way causes secondary heating and further decomposition to occur. I usually start using the manure after it has been composted for a total time of between three and six months.

● Cow Manure

As with horse manure, cow manure should be composted with straw before being used. Its nutrient content will depend on the diet supplied to the cows and the amount of straw mixed with it prior to composting.

SCREEN BLOCK MANURE CONTAINER

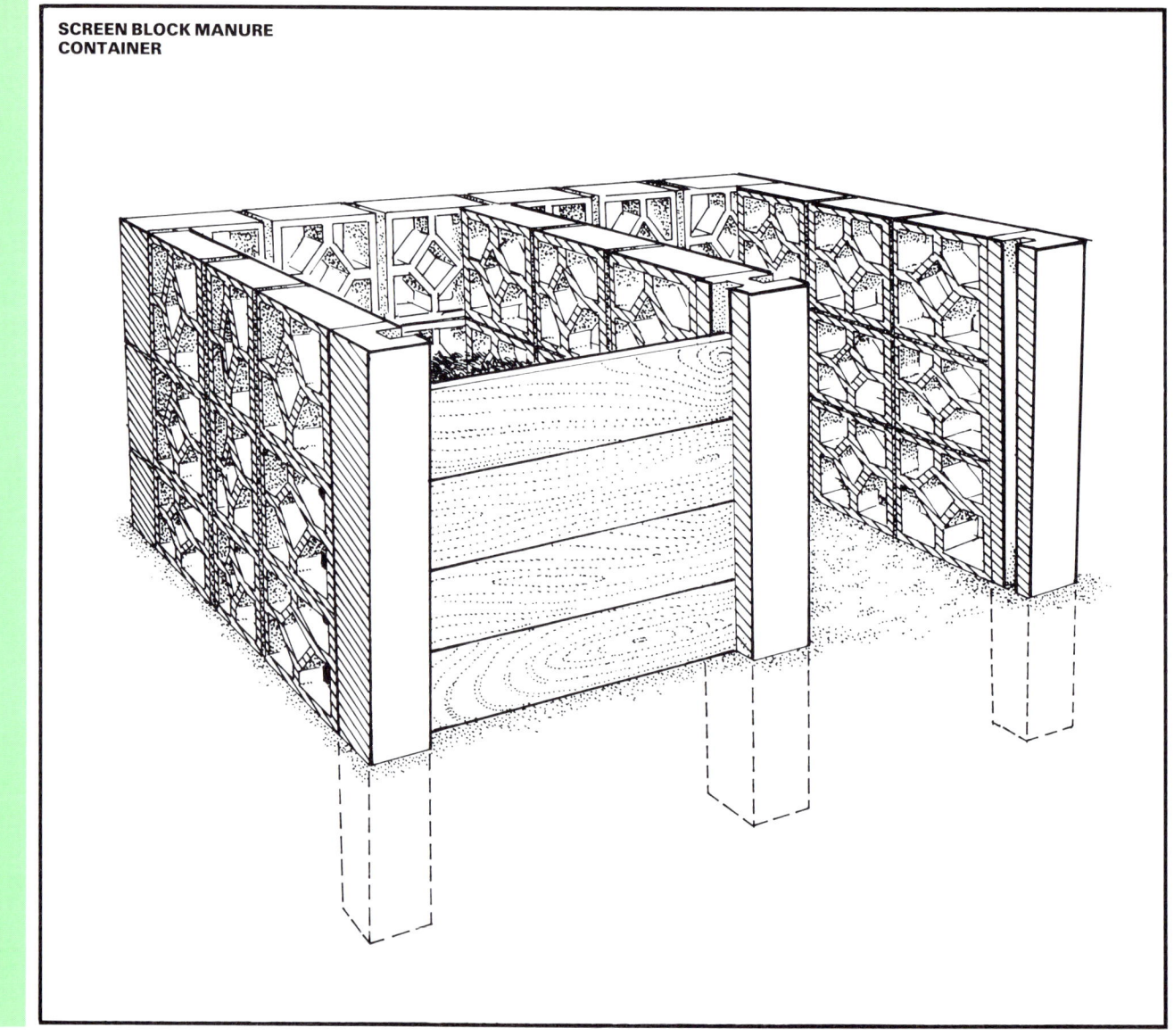

● Pigeon Manure

This is a very concentrated manure that should not be applied directly to crops. One way of making use of pigeon manure is to hoe it into the soil around comfrey plants. Some scorching of the leaves may take place but no serious harm should be done provided that it is only used on well established plants. Another method of using this manure that could be tried is to build a compost heap consisting of layers of damp straw with pigeon manure scattered on as an activator.

● Pig Manure

Manure from pigs that are fed on manufactured food will contain copper. For this reason I would not recommend its use in the garden.

Organic Fertilisers

Although ground minerals cannot really be described as 'organic', I have included them under this heading because they are permitted in organic gardening.

Organic gardens should not require the regular application of concentrated fertilisers that are used in inorganic gardening. Removal of nutrients will be cut to a minimum if the uneaten parts of plants, eg tomato haulm, are recycled via the compost heap. Manure brought into the garden will eventually rot down and release nutrients which will help to replace those taken from the soil by crops. Some soils may be deficient in certain plant foods, either because they are naturally so or because of previous misuse, and may therefore benefit from the addition of concentrated organic fertilisers.

● Blood, Fish and Bonemeal

When bought from a normal retail outlet, this fertiliser usually contains a chemical form of potassium. The HDRA sells blood, fish and bonemeal without this added chemical and, in this case, the fertiliser provides mainly nitrogen and phosphorus. The blood component of this mixture provides rapidly available nitrogen and this is not really in line with organic principles. *Approximate application rate: 4oz/sq yd.*

● Bonemeal

Although this fertiliser contains some nitrogen, it is used mainly for its supply of phosphorus. It provides a lasting supply of this plant food, the fineness of grinding determining the rate of release. *Approximate application rate: 4oz/sq yd.*

● Dried Blood

This is an expensive nitrogen fertiliser with a rapid action referred to under blood, fish and bonemeal.

● Calcified Seaweed (Lithothamnium calcareum)

Opinions about this product vary somewhat in the organic movement. Some people say that it is simply an expensive form of calcium, while others consider it a valuable fertiliser containing magnesium and trace elements. It is widely used on the granite soils of Brittany. I use calcified seaweed myself, but I have never done any trials, using another form of calcium as a control, to see whether it has any special benefits on my soil.

● Rock Potash

Another rather controversial organic fertiliser, I am afraid. On the Continent, various types of rock dust are used to provide a supply of potassium for organic systems. Recently, a ground-up form of Andularian shale, known as rock potash, has become available in Britain. Some growers are willing to spend money on large quantities of this fertiliser because of the beneficial effect they believe it has on their crops. On the other hand, I have heard it said that although this mineral does contain potassium, it would take an atom bomb to release it for the use of plants. I can only suggest that gardeners with potassium-deficient soils should test the fertiliser for themselves by applying it to part of their land and then checking the subsequent yields. *Approximate application rate: 8oz/sq yd.*

● Rock Phosphate

This is available as 'Gafsa', for use on soils with a pH below 7 and 'Reddzlaag', for use on alkaline soils. It may be an advantage to add rock phosphate to composting material as it is being built into a heap, rather than apply it directly to the soil. The idea behind this procedure is that the acids formed during composting will react with the rock phosphate and make it more readily available to plants. Gardeners will find that bonemeal is easier to buy than rock phosphate.

Left:
Rotted manure in screen block New Zealand Box. The black polythene lining has been removed.

● **Seaweed Meal**

Seaweed meal is an expensive fertiliser if it is judged by the amount of major plant foods that it contains, but its overall effect, especially on soils with low levels of organic matter, can be very beneficial. The alginates present in seaweed provide nourishment for bacteria and therefore increase the biological activity in the soil. Seaweed also contains a wide range of trace elements. *Apply in the autumn at approximately 4oz/sq yd.*

● **Liquid Seaweed Extracts**

At one time, the beneficial effects of these products was thought to be due to their trace element content. Even generous applications of liquid seaweed will not supply sufficient quantities of these elements to make up for a deficient soil however, and so there must be other factors involved. It seems that plant growth regulators are mainly responsible for the increased yields and crop quality produced by seaweed extracts. These products are likely to give the most marked effect when used on crops that have been given less than ideal growing conditions.

Mineral Deficiencies

Deficiency symptoms in plants do not necessarily indicate a corresponding lack of minerals in the soil. It may well be that the soil contains an adequate supply of the particular element required, but that unfavourable conditions in the soil are making it unavailable to plants. Hopefully, the advice given in various parts of this book will help the reader to create a fertile soil and avoid frequent reference to the following table.

Element	Deficiency Symptoms	Likely Cause/Remedy
Nitrogen	Slow growth, small light green or yellow leaves and poor plant development	Occurs on soils containing low levels of organic matter, therefore dressings of compost/manure should be increased
Phosphorus	Slow growth, resulting in small plants. Leaves may be tinted a bronze or dull purple colour, especially those of sweet corn	May be due to a low level of biological activity in the soil. Naturally deficient soils can be treated with bone meal or rock phosphate
Potassium	Margins of older leaves suffer greyish-brown scorching, Chocolate Spot may appear on broad beans	Shortages may be found on light, shallow soils and a possible remedy is the application of rock potash (*see remarks about this substance under 'Organic Fertilisers'*). Bringing manure into a garden will, of course, enrich the soil with potassium
Calcium	Crops may develop symptoms due to low pH or lack of calcium. Blossom End Rot of tomatoes and Bitter Pit in apples are diseases related to lack of calcium	Calcium can be supplied and the pH raised by applying ground limestone or calcified seaweed
Magnesium	Usually shows on older leaves as yellowing between the veins	Can be caused by excessive use of soluble potassium fertilisers. This element may be supplied in the form of dolomitic limestone
Boron	Death of growing points and hollow stems of brassicas, cauliflowers with brown or undeveloped curds	Usually caused by applying too much lime — avoid this in the future. A dressing of seaweed meal will supply some boron
Manganese	Marsh Spot in peas is an obvious symptom and can be recognised by the brown spots which develop in the actual seeds	High levels of calcium will 'lock up' manganese and so overliming should be avoided

Gardeners wishing to obtain detailed information about their own soil may be interested in the soil analysis service offered by Elm Farm Research Centre (address at the back of this book). The analysis is appropriate to the needs of organic growers and will provide information about the present state of the soil and advice about its future treatment.

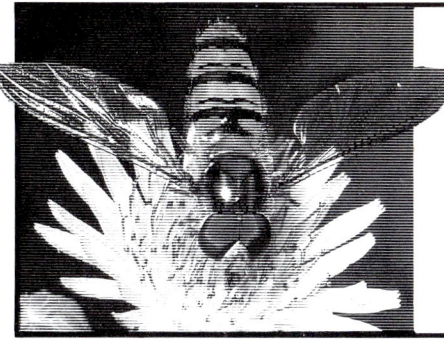

7 Green Manuring

A green manure crop is one that is grown for incorporation into the soil rather than human consumption. The green manure that almost every gardener has heard of is mustard, but others such as fodder radish and buckwheat are less well known.

Allowing weeds to colonise bare soil could be regarded as a form of green manuring, but this does have several disadvantages. Annual weeds will easily set seed and cause trouble for the future. Once perennial weeds such as docks and couch become established, they are troublesome to get rid of. The bulk of material produced by self-sown weeds will not compare very favourably with that produced by properly grown green manures.

Advantages of Green Manuring

● Increased Biological Activity in the Soil

Beneficial micro-organisms and earthworms will be encouraged by covering the soil with a green manure crop rather than leaving it bare for long periods. When the crop is finally incorporated into the soil, there will be a great increase in biological activity as it decays.

● Reduced Loss of Plant Foods by Leaching

It is possible for heavy winter rain to wash nutrients through the soil and out of reach of plant roots. Over-wintering green manures can be used to collect these plant foods and store them for use by a following crop. The nutrients will, of course, be released when the green manure decays after incorporation into the soil.

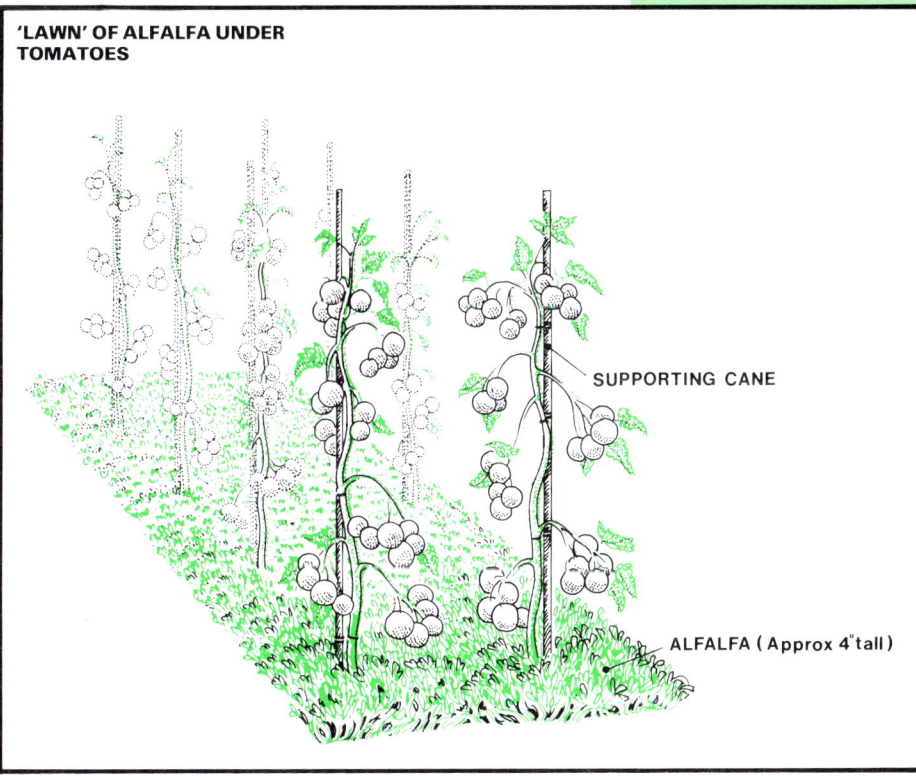

'LAWN' OF ALFALFA UNDER TOMATOES

SUPPORTING CANE

ALFALFA (Approx 4" tall)

● Reduced Weed Growth

Some green manures are very good at suppressing weeds, provided that they are sown at the correct time. I have found that a 'lawn' of alfalfa, sown beneath tomato plants, is very effective for this purpose. The alfalfa seed was not sown until midsummer, by which time I had killed the early crop of weeds by hoeing.

● Increased Organic Matter

As the name suggests, green manures are usually turned into the soil while they are still green and sappy. The rate at which they decay is much more rapid than that of more woody material, and so their contribution to soil organic matter is most important in the short term.

● Nitrogen Fixation

Leguminous green manures have the ability, aided by bacteria in their root nodules, to make use of nitrogen from the air. Much of the nitrogen fixed in this way should be available to a following crop.

One problem with green manures is that they take up space where vegetables could otherwise be grown. In a small garden, where space is at a premium, this difficulty can be overcome by sowing suitable green manures in spring or autumn, when part of the garden would normally be empty, or by undersowing tall crops.

Methods of Rotting Down Green Manure Crops

● Turning into the Soil

This can be done by hand or with a mechanical cultivator, but the crop should not be buried deeply. Ideally, it should be thoroughly broken up and mixed with the top few inches of soil, where there is an adequate supply of air for rapid decomposition. Cutting tall green manures with a mower prior to incorporation will make the task easier. As I no longer dig my garden, I use hoeing and mulching to kill off my green manures.

● Mulching

Lightproof mulches such as black polythene can be used to kill a green manure crop and cause it to be taken into the soil by earthworms. The technique is similar to that described for killing weeds in Chapter 9. One way of ensuring that a mulch is available for killing off a green manure is by fitting such a crop into the garden rotation just before no-dig potatoes. I hoe through the soil before planting the seed potatoes and then rely

PULLING UP GREEN MANURE FOR COMPOSTING

on a thick organic mulch to prevent any re-growth of the green manure.

● Removal for Composting

Green manures that have been left to become woody are not suitable for direct incorporation into the soil because their decomposition would be too slow. A much better way of dealing with such crops is to pull them up and compost them in a bin. Another alternative would be to use the tops of the plants for mulching.

Varieties of Green Manures Suitable for Gardeners

● Agricultural Chicory

This is a deep-rooting but inedible type of chicory that is only suitable for green manuring. Although it is usually mixed with other green manures, it can be used alone to help restore exhausted soil. I grew this crop in my own garden some time

**TURNING GREEN MANURE
INTO THE SOIL WITH A
CULTIVATOR**

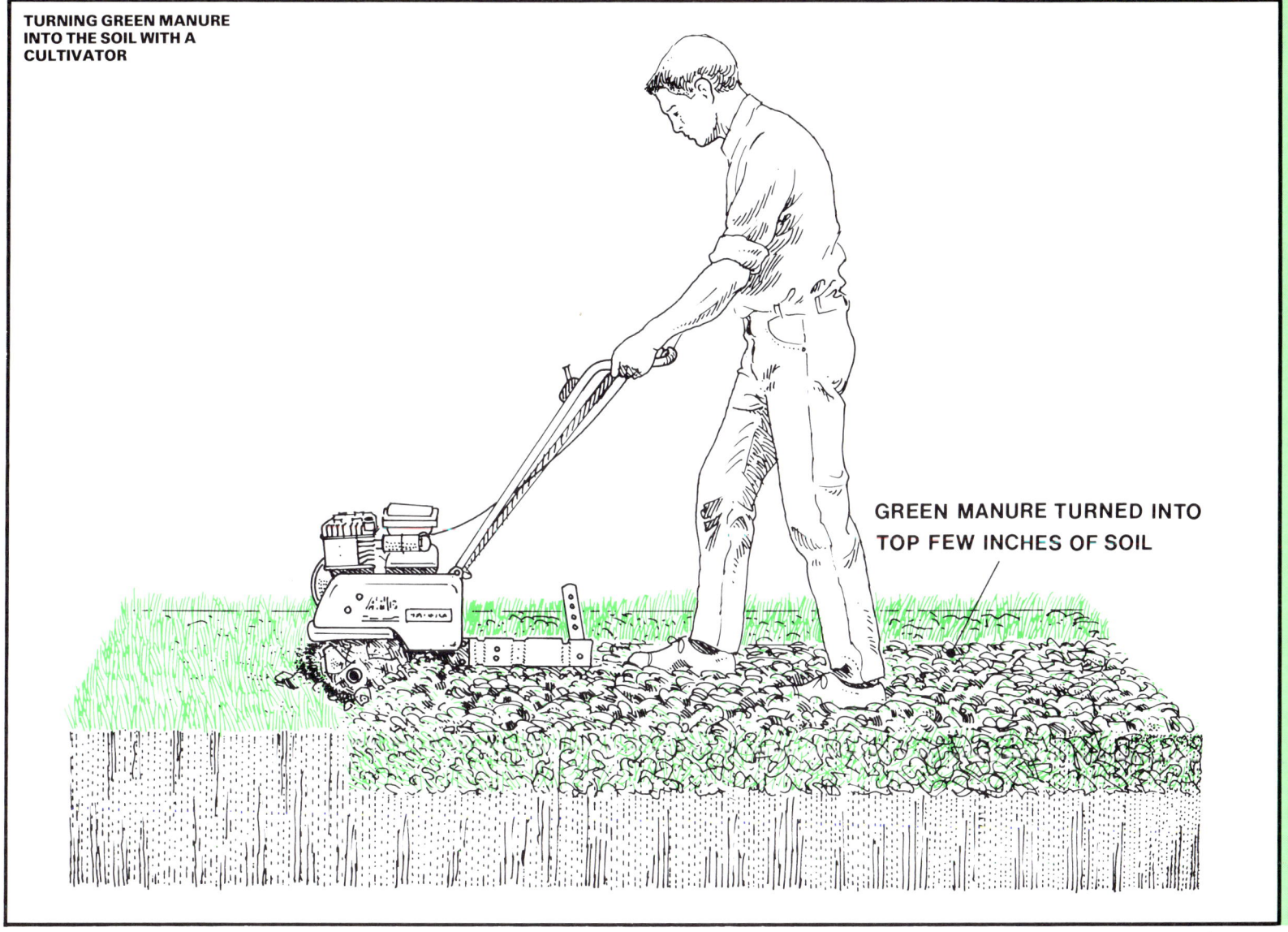

GREEN MANURE TURNED INTO
TOP FEW INCHES OF SOIL

ago and did have some difficulty in killing it off. The problem was that the large amount of food stored in the roots enabled the chicory to re-grow several times after being cut with a hoe. Gardeners who use a mechanical cultivator to break up and incorporate their green manures may find this re-growth is not a problem.

● Alfalfa

Also known as lucerne, this plant is used as a fodder crop in agriculture. Being very deep-rooting, alfalfa has good drought resistance and, when used as a green manure, it provides a large range of nutrients for the subsequent crop. If plenty of space is available, alfalfa can be grown in the same place for several years to provide mulching or composting material. Although it is a legume, alfalfa is not always able to fix nitrogen because the necessary bacteria are not present in most British soils. This deficiency can be overcome by innoculating the seed with the correct bacteria before sowing. I have been very impressed with alfalfa since I started using it as a green manure. Once established, it provides good, weed-smothering ground cover, a large bulk of green material above ground and a lot of deep roots. It is only fair to warn however, that these roots are very tough and cutting through them with a hoe does require a certain amount of effort.

● Buckwheat

This is a summer-sown green manure with flowers that are very attractive to bees and hoverflies. Its rapid growth and deep roots make it a valuable crop if space is available in the garden during the main growing season.

● Clover

There are several varieties of this leguminous plant suitable for green manuring:

Alsike
A Canadian variety that can be used on poor, acid soils and which will survive extremes of temperature.

Essex Red
An excellent green manure for producing a mass of roots and a good bulk of green material.

White
A strong-growing variety that will compete well with weeds.

On my allotment, where space is not at a premium, I grow clover as part of the crop rotation. I sow it in the spring, and the summer growth is sufficient for several cuts of mulching

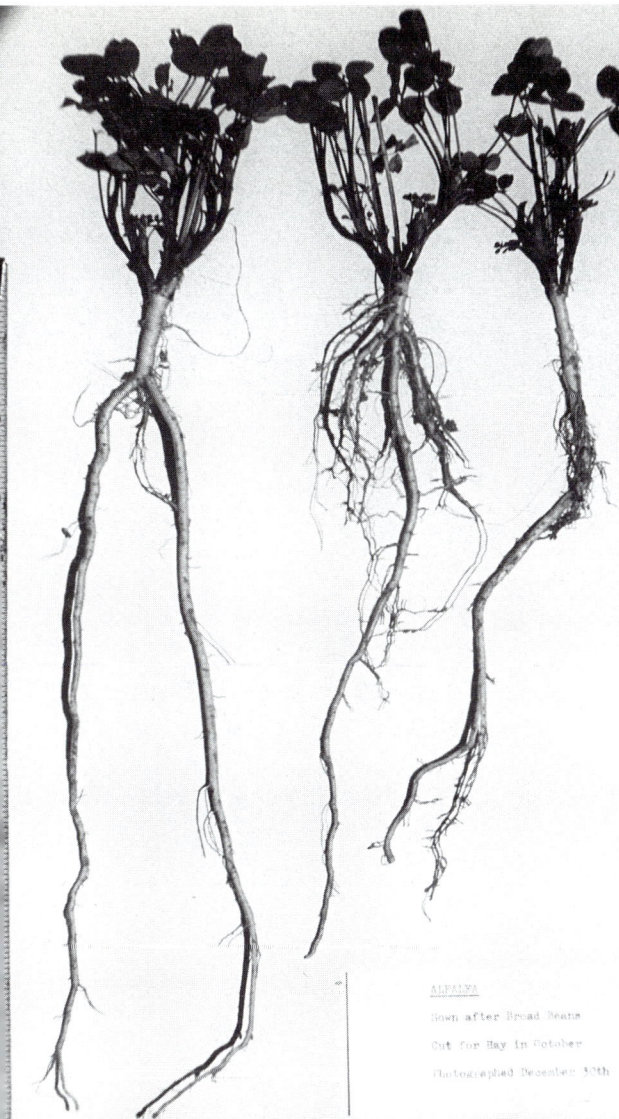

ALFALFA

Sown after Broad Beans

Cut for Hay in October

Photographed December 30th

material. Growing the clover prior to potatoes means that it can be killed off with a thick mulch.

● Fodder Radish

As the name implies, fodder radish can provide suitable food for animals such as sheep and goats. It is very fast growing, provided that it is not sown too late in the season.

● Grazing Rye

Of the green manures that I have grown, I have found rye to be the best for smothering weeds. It is so good in fact that my attempts to produce a mixed green manure crop of rye and clover have never been successful. Although I left a gap of 9in between the rows of rye and then broadcast the clover seed, the clover never competed well enough to become established. Grazing rye has a very extensive root system which is of great benefit to soil structure. An autumn-sown crop will provide good soil cover for the winter and further growth in the spring.

● Lupins

Known as the bitter lupin, this annual plant has the advantage of fixing nitrogen. It can be grown on infertile, acid soils where other green manures would not be suitable. Being a summer

Facing page, top:
Agricultural Chicory.

Facing page, bottom:
Alfalfa.

Left:
Alfalfa roots.

Below:
Alsike Clover.

Right:
Fodder Radish.

Far right:
These young grazing rye plants have already produced an extensive root system.

crop, lupins do have to be fitted carefully into the garden rotation to avoid reducing the space available for vegetables. I would suggest sowing lupins in ground that has been prepared for sweet corn or tomatoes, and then cutting them for compost material when the edible crops need the space.

● Mustard

A fast growing, but shallow rooting green manure that is suitable for summer use. It is unable to fix nitrogen and does present a problem in connection with the disease clubroot. The main advantage of mustard is that it will produce a large amount of foliage in just a few weeks.

● Sunflowers

An inexpensive supply of sunflower seed for green manuring can be obtained from a pet shop. Sunflowers are very good for producing a large supply of composting material from spare ground. Cutting the plants when they are 3 to 4ft high and then sowing another sunflower crop will prevent the stems

Far left:
Agricultural Lupins produce attractive spikes of flowers.

Below:
Mustard.

becoming thick and woody. Some years ago I sowed sunflowers 1ft apart each way on an area of ground measuring 15ft × 15ft and allowed them to grow for a whole season. The result was a rather spectacular 'forest' of plants with large flower heads. Removing the soil from the roots and breaking up the stems before composting was not easy, however. Perhaps putting the stems through a compost shredder and leaving the roots in the ground to rot would have been a better idea.

● Winter Tares

A very useful, nitrogen-fixing green manure that can be sown in late summer to give ground cover during the winter. Tares can also be sown in the spring and will help to suppress weeds.

I have described the green manures (right) because they are suitable for use in the garden and the seed is relatively easy to obtain. Other varieties are available but are either used mainly in farming or have not been tested fully for use in Britain.

Green Manure	Sowing Time	Approx Area Covered by 8oz of Seed	Sowing Method
Agricultural Chicory	Any time during growing season	70sq ft	Broadcast
Alfalfa	As above	500sq ft	Broadcast
Buckwheat	May to July	300sq ft	Broadcast or in Drills
Clover	Spring or late Summer	500sq ft	Broadcast
Fodder Radish	Late Summer	500sq ft	Broadcast or in Drills
Grazing Rye	Autumn	250sq ft	Broadcast or in Drills
Lupins	April to July	200sq ft	In Drills
Mustard	Summer	600sq ft	Broadcast
Winter Tares	Spring or Autumn	200sq ft	In Drills

Right:
Winter Tares.

8
Comfrey

Comfrey is a deep-rooting perennial herb that is grown for medicinal use and as a green manure. As I am not qualified to comment on its healing properties, the description of comfrey in this book will be limited to its use in the garden.

The best variety of comfrey for gardeners is Bocking No 14 because this will give a high yield and is unlikely to set seed. An initial supply of plants can be bought through the post from the HDRA, and then the stock increased by taking root cuttings once the original plants are well established. Comfrey is not rotated around the garden like other green manures, but should be planted in a permanent position. This site should be chosen carefully as comfrey's deep roots make it a difficult plant to get rid of if it is grown in the wrong place. Cuttings may be planted at any time during the growing season at a spacing of 2ft apart with 2ft between rows. Although comfrey will produce its best yield if grown in full sun and in fertile soil, it will still produce a useful amount of foliage in less ideal conditions. In my own garden I have comfrey growing between a concrete path and a privet hedge. This uses land that could not be used for growing crops and still provides a good supply of comfrey leaves.

Newly planted comfrey should be allowed to establish itself for a season before the foliage is cut. Flower stems will be produced in the summer and these should be removed. Comfrey will respond well to a regular supply of animal manure, even if this is used without first being composted. Rust is about the only disease problem likely to be encountered when growing comfrey. The appearance of the disease seems to be related to a nutritional deficiency — probably potassium. Comfrey rust was present on a few of the plants in my garden some years ago, but the plants all appear to be healthy now. The comfrey plants recovered after being fed with seaweed meal,

Right:
Comfrey cuttings . . .

Far right:
. . . planted in the soil.

calcified seaweed and stable manure, which were used to improve the rather poor soil at the base of the privet hedge.

The growth of well-fed comfrey is quite remarkable and it should be possible to harvest the leaves four or five times during a season. This should be done by cutting off the foliage just above ground level, being careful not to pull up any pieces of root. Its high nitrogen content and readiness to decay make comfrey a versatile source of plant foods that does not need prior composting.

Uses for Comfrey in the Garden

● Mulching

A layer of comfrey leaves placed on the soil will help to retain moisture and will also provide plant foods as decomposition occurs. Considerable shrinkage will take place as the comfrey dries in the sun, and so a thick layer will be required if weed suppression is the reason for applying the mulch. An alternative method of providing a thick mulch is to use a thin layer of comfrey leaves covered with grass mowings or hay. In my experience, such a mulch protects and improves the texture of the soil surface, encourages earthworms, provides a steady supply of nutrients and protects surface roots. Information about growing no-dig potatoes using comfrey is given in Chapter 9.

Left:
Cutting comfrey with shears . . .

Overleaf:
. . . and mulching around tomato plants.

● In Planting Holes

Wilted comfrey leaves can be used to line planting holes when putting in crops such as tomatoes. Obviously, an oversize hole has to be dug to accommodate the comfrey and care should be taken not to include any pieces of root because these would grow into unwanted comfrey plants. Using a layer of comfrey leaves in a potato trench to provide nutrients and reduce potato scab is recommended by Lawrence Hills, but I have not tried this method myself as I no longer dig such trenches.

● In the Compost Heap

Comfrey contains far too much water to be composted on its own in a normal container. It can be used, however, to provide moisture by incorporating it into what would otherwise be a dry heap.

● Comfrey Liquid Manure

Its high moisture content and the speed with which it breaks down means that comfrey is well suited to the production of liquid manure. The resulting comfrey liquid is rich in potassium and can therefore be used to feed crops such as tomatoes. The black residue left in the container after all the comfrey liquid has run off can either be added to the compost heap or used as a mulch.

Although a water butt is used as a container in the two methods described below, a smaller container, such as a plastic bucket, would obviously be more suitable if only a small quantity of comfrey is available.

● Method 1

1. Place a sufficient thickness of gravel in the bottom of a water butt to just cover the outlet. The stones will act as a coarse filter and prevent comfrey leaves blocking the tap. Another advantage of this layer is that it will reduce the volume of liquid that cannot be drained off via the tap.
2. As water butt taps are sited near the base, placing a reasonable size container under the tap is difficult. The problem can be overcome either by standing the butt on bricks or by digging a small hole in the ground beneath the tap.
3. Fill the water butt with all the available comfrey. The leaves should be used fresh, rather than wilted, otherwise there will be very little liquid to drip out.
4. Place weights such as broken paving slabs on top of the comfrey.

It should be possible to drain off a dark coloured liquid after a few weeks and this needs to be diluted with about 10 parts of water before being used.

I usually make comfrey liquid in the autumn and this means that the comfrey has several months to decay and produce liquid manure for the next season.

● Method 2

This method is more suitable for small amounts of comfrey, but does produce a much stronger smell than Method 1.

1. Prepare a water butt as in Method 1.
2. Place comfrey leaves in the container and then fill up with water. The HDRA recommends using 7lb of leaves for every 10gal of water.
3. Allow the mixture to ferment until the comfrey decomposes, about four weeks.
4. Drain off the liquid and use undiluted.

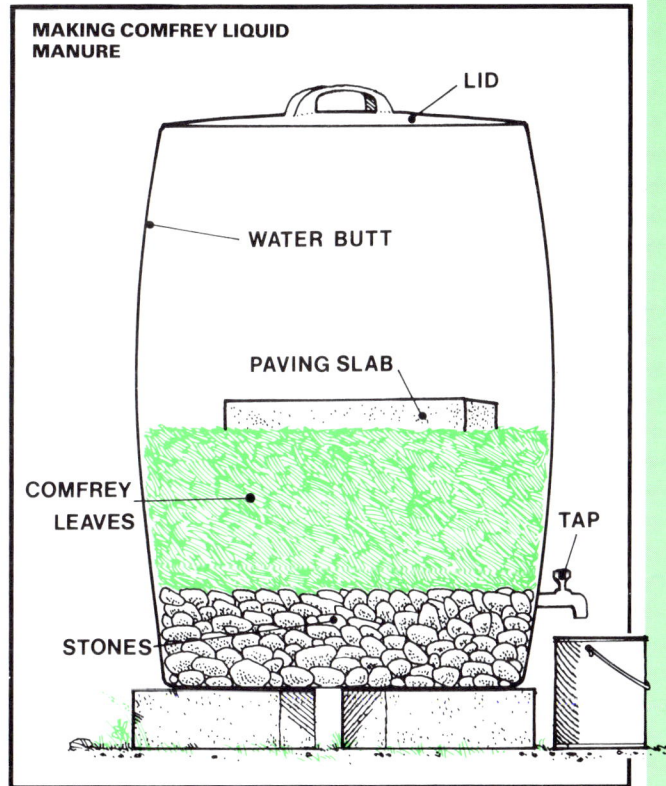

MAKING COMFREY LIQUID MANURE

LID

WATER BUTT

PAVING SLAB

COMFREY LEAVES

TAP

STONES

Right:
**Pouring comfrey liquid from
a water butt.**

If liquid manure made by either of the above methods is to be applied using a watering can with a rose, further filtration through an old pair of tights is advisable.

● **Comfrey Peat**
The plant foods taken up from the soil by comfrey can be used to enrich potting mixtures. One way of achieving this is by composting the comfrey with peat and then using the finished product, either on its own or with other components, for potting. Peat has the ability to absorb plant nutrients and moisture as they are released from the comfrey, and will give an open textue to the mixture. Of course, the drier the peat, the more moisture it will be able to absorb from the comfrey.

A normal composting container may be used to make comfrey peat, but I find that a plastic dustbin is quite suitable for the amount that I produce. It must be remembered, however, that plastic dustbins do not allow evaporation and so the mixture may easily become waterlogged. Using dry peat and well wilted comfrey will overcome this problem.

● **Method**
1. Cut the comfrey and allow it to wilt. Spreading out the leaves on concrete in full sun is the quickest method of reducing their water content, but the British climate does not always make this possible.
2. Spread a 2in layer of sedge peat in the dustbin and then add a 4in layer of comfrey. Dust the surface of the comfrey with calcified seaweed or ground limestone.

3. Build up more layers until either the bin is full or the comfrey is used up.
4. Leave the mixture to decay for about three weeks and then tip it out of the bin. It will be obvious at this stage if the mixture is too wet and, if this is the case, it can be left to dry in the sun.
5. Replace the mixture in the bin for further composting.

After a total time of about six weeks the comfrey leaves should have decomposed and been absorbed by the peat. It is likely that there will be some skeletal remains of the comfrey stems at this stage, but these may be sieved out before the comfrey peat is used. Making comfrey peat in late summer allows for several months of composting before it is required for use in spring potting mixtures.

The proportions of comfrey and peat given above should be regarded only as a guide. It is not possible to give an exact mathematical formula because the water content, and therefore the volume of comfrey varies so much according to how long it is wilted. Fortunately, the ratio is not critical and a little experimenting should produce a successful technique. The use of comfrey peat is covered in Chapter 11.

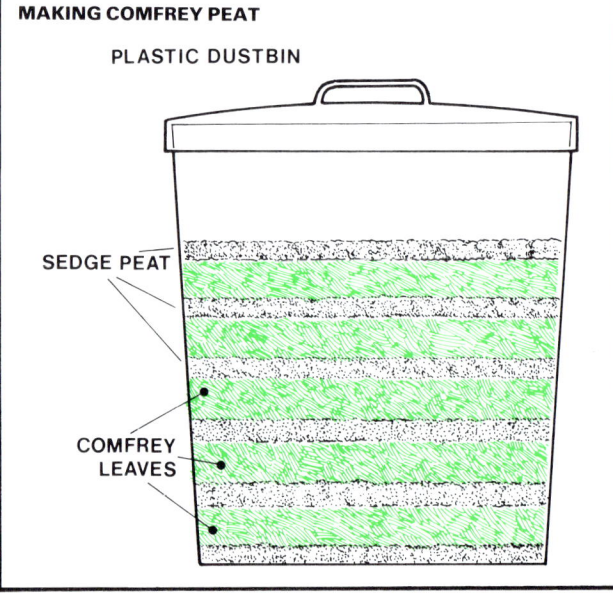

MAKING COMFREY PEAT

PLASTIC DUSTBIN

SEDGE PEAT

COMFREY LEAVES

9 Mulching

The word mulch is used in gardening to describe a layer of material placed on the surface of the soil to reduce the evaporation of moisture. The materials that can be used for this purpose vary from lawn mowings to black polythene and the technique of mulching is so versatile that a full chapter of this book has been devoted to its description.

A good example of natural mulching can be found on the floor of a forest where dead leaves accumulate. The leaves slowly decay into leafmould and this forms a barrier which protects the surface roots of the trees. Eventually, the leaves decay completely thus recycling the nutrients they contain.

Advantages of Using a Mulch

If carefully chosen and applied at the correct time, mulches will have the following benefits for the gardener.
● Evaporation from the soil surface will be reduced or prevented
● Existing weeds may be killed, and further weed growth restricted or prevented
● As a consequence of restricted weed growth, hoeing, which can damage the surface roots of crops, is not necessary
● Biological activity in the soil surface will be enhanced and the surface roots of plants encouraged by the micro climate created by the mulch
● Protection will be given against damage to the soil surface by heavy rain and the use of a hose
● Mulches such as comfrey and lawn mowings will decay into the soil and provide plant foods
● The greenhouse effect produced by clear polythene will warm up the soil

● When growing potatoes, a mulch can be used instead of the usual earthing-up process, to exclude light and prevent the tubers turning green
● Thermal insulation. This can be an advantage or disadvantage, according to when the mulch is applied, because a mulch applied to a warm soil will keep it warm and a mulch spread on a cold soil will tend to prevent it warming up.

Disadvantages of Mulching

● Cost: obviously, this does not apply to material such as newspaper and cardboard which can be obtained free
● Slugs may be attracted to the mulch and cause damage to crops such as potatoes
● Although polythene prevents evaporation from the soil surface, moisture will still be lost because of the transpiration of plants. As polythene will keep the rain off the soil, it must be either sloped or perforated to direct water to the plants' roots
● Some mulches will reflect some of the radiant heat from the sun which would normally reach, and therefore warm up, bare soil. This effect is more pronounced early in the season when the soil is not shaded by plant leaves. Later, as plants grow and prevent more sunshine reaching the soil anyway, there will be less temperature difference between mulched and unmulched ground.

Materials for Mulching

● **Leafmould**
Details of how to make leafmould will be found in Chapter 4. Unless a very thick layer of leafmould is used, weed suppression

is unlikely to be very effective. It is an excellent source of organic matter however, and will greatly improve the physical condition of the soil both initially and for some time in the future.

● Shredded Bark

This can be used as a decorative mulch in the ornamental garden, for example beneath rhododendrons and conifers. Its use in the vegetable garden, where economic considerations play a greater part, is doubtful because of the high cost.

● Peat

As with shredded bark, cost usually excludes peat from use as a mulch in the vegetable garden. It can be substituted for straw however, for use under strawberries to keep the fruit off the ground.

● Lawn Mowings

Most gardeners will have a supply of this free mulching material. Care must be taken if lawn mowings are obtained from someone else because of the possibility of contamination with weedkillers. Another point to bear in mind when using a mulch containing lawn mowings is the possibility of attracting slugs.

● Straw

There are a number of disadvantages that make fresh straw far from ideal for use as a mulching material. Unless organically grown, the straw will be contaminated with agricultural chemicals which may wash into the soil and on to crops. The heat produced in composting, especially if the straw contains animal manure, would normally help to reduce the levels of these chemicals. A mulch of straw will keep the soil much cooler than would be the case without such a covering and will therefore slow down the development and ripening of crops. Straw is not as easy for earthworms to take into the soil as are other organic mulches and so may have to be removed for composting at the end of the season. During a trial of various mulching materials conducted by the HDRA, plants grown through a straw mulch yielded unfavourably when compared with those grown both in bare soil and through other mulches.

● Comfrey

If comfrey is being grown as a green manure crop, one of the ways in which it can be used is as a mulch. If a comfrey mulch is kept damp, either because of weather conditions or because of a dense canopy of foliage above it, it will rot down rapidly and add liquid manure to the soil. This means that thin comfrey mulches will not last very long on the soil surface. A no-dig method of growing potatoes using comfrey as a mulch is described later in this chapter.

Sheet Mulches

The various mulches just described are fairly easily penetrated from above by rain, and from below by weeds. The following materials are used in sheet form and are therefore more resistant to penetration.

● Newspaper

A thick covering of newspaper is very good for killing off weeds and has the advantage of nil cost, but the ground below such a covering can become very dry. Lawn mowings can be spread on top of newspaper to keep it in place and such a combination will form an excellent weed-suppressing mulch.

● Cardboard

Cardboard rots into the soil more quickly than does newspaper and does not blow about so much when it is being laid, but in other respects can be treated in a similar fashion.

● Black Polythene

Polythene is unlike the materials previously described because it will not decay into the soil and supply organic matter or plant foods. It is manufactured in various thicknesses and the one chosen should be determined by the use to which the polythene will be put. If the polythene sheet is simply to be used to kill weeds it may be worthwhile to use a heavy gauge, eg 500g, so that the sheet may be reused several times. On the other hand, if planting holes are to be made through the sheet and it is to be

Far left:
Lawn mowings are a useful mulching material.

Left:
Cardboard can be used as an alternative to newspaper for mulching.

scrapped at the end of the season, a much thinner gauge, eg 200g, should be used. Cost is a major disadvantage of black polythene but it is a very easy material to use and it is very effective for killing weeds.

● **Clear Polythene**

It may be possible to obtain second-hand clear polythene that has been used for wrapping such things as carpet. Another source of supply is the polythene that is scrapped after use on cloches and polytunnels. Clear polythene does not have the light-excluding properties of other mulches and will therefore not have the same weed-killing effect. It has a considerable soil-warming effect however, and can therefore be used to make plants crop earlier in the season, eg early potatoes. Early in the season, germination of seeds such as carrots can be improved by pre-warming the soil with a sheet of clear polythene that has been left in place for a few weeks.

The above list is not an exhaustive one but does provide a guide to the most commonly-used mulching materials. Other materials that can be applied as a mulch include compost, manures and hay cut from green manures.

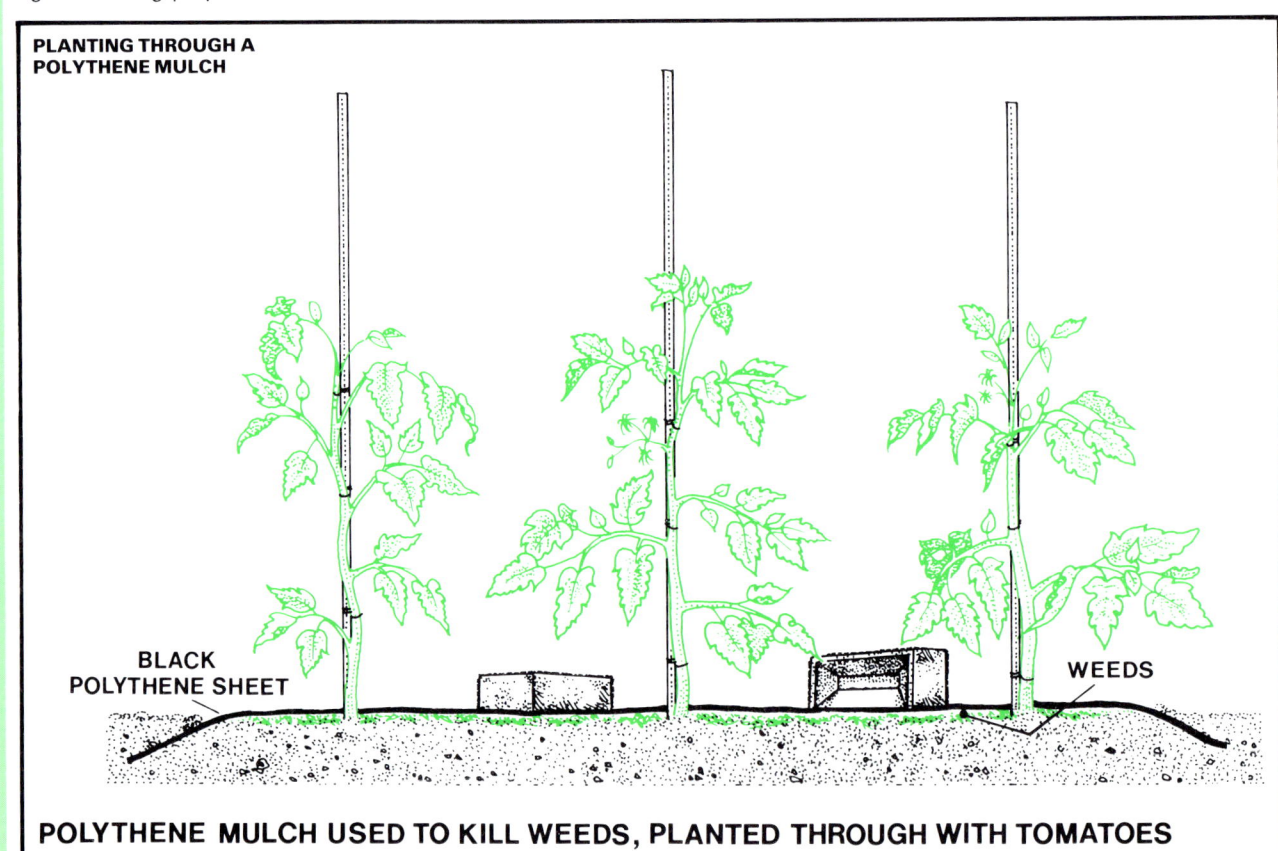

PLANTING THROUGH A POLYTHENE MULCH

BLACK POLYTHENE SHEET

WEEDS

POLYTHENE MULCH USED TO KILL WEEDS, PLANTED THROUGH WITH TOMATOES

Methods of Using a Mulch

Mulches can be used on many different crops and in a variety of ways. It is hoped that the two detailed examples given below will enable the reader to understand the technique and adapt it for personal use.

EXAMPLE 1 — CLEARING UNCULTIVATED GROUND

The sight of an overgrown garden or allotment and the thought of the work involved in bringing it back into cultivation can be very intimidating. Soil that is covered with a large variety of tall, healthy weeds is likely to be very fertile however, and it is well worth the effort required to bring it back into cultivation. It is easy to spot allotments that have been worked out and recently abandoned because the poor, stunted weed growth shows low fertility. Most gardeners faced with overgrown ground resort either to herbicides or digging to remove the weeds. The residues left by herbicides and the hard work involved in digging can both be avoided by the use of a light-excluding mulch. My own allotment, which is shown in the photographs, was brought back into cultivation by this method.

● **Black Polythene**

Before purchasing the polythene it is necessary to decided whether or not crops are going to be planted through it. As previously mentioned, if holes are not to be cut through it, heavy-duty polythene should be re-useable, but if crops are to be planted through the sheet a thinner gauge should be chosen.

1. Cut down tall weeds with a scythe or use a mechanical cultivator to turn them into the surface of the soil.
2. Cover with black polythene.
3. Hold the polythene down by burying the edges, weighing down with bricks or a combination of both. With large sheets to avoid treading on the polythene and damaging it, bricks should be placed on the polythene as it is unrolled.

As the weeds beneath them rot down, the bricks are likely to damage the polythene. This damage can be reduced either by placing newspapers directly below the bricks or by substituting them with polythene bags filled with sand or soil. When using a lightproof mulch to kill weeds, it is important to cover as large an area as possible. If paths are left between mulching sheets, weeds such as bindweed and couch grass will be able to produce food to keep their roots alive under the mulch. If crops are to be planted through the polythene, this can be done by cutting two slits at right angles through it and using a trowel to make a planting hole. If watering becomes necessary, it must be done through this hole and any weeds growing up through it

Left:
Clear polythene used to raise the soil temperature for early potatoes.

Below left:
Slits are cut in the polythene to allow the potato tops to grow through.

should be pulled out by hand. Obviously, it will be necessary to walk on the polythene for watering the plants and for picking crops, but as the thin polythene would be scrapped at the end of the season anyway, the damage caused is not too important.

Previous page:
The weeds on my allotment were 'turned in' with a mechanical cultivator . . .

Inset:
. . . thin black polythene was laid, and crops planted.

Far left:
PLANTING THROUGH BLACK POLYTHENE: run over ground with cultivator.

Left:
Lay black polythene. (It is not really necessary to use this many stones to hold down the polythene.)

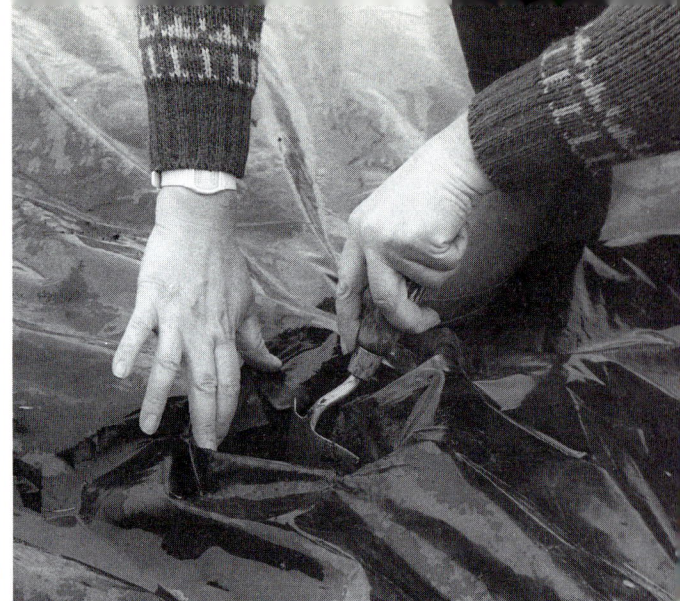

Far left:
Cut two slits to form a cross in the polythene.

Facing page, top:
Make a planting hole with a trowel.

Facing page, bottom:
Put the plant in position . . .

Left:
. . . and firm into place.

Right:
MULCHING WITH NEWSPAPER: an overgrown allotment can be rather daunting.

Below:
Cut the weeds with a lawn mower . . .

Below right:
. . . lay overlapped sheets of wet newspaper on the ground . . .

● Newspaper

1. Cut down tall weeds with a scythe or lawnmower and remove them.
2. Newspaper is much more fragile than polythene and so a thickness of several sheets must be used. If plenty of newspaper is available, simply open up the paper and use the complete edition.
3. Dipping in water will make the newspaper easier to lay because it will prevent the wind blowing it away so readily.
4. An overlap of a couple of inches should be used to help prevent weeds pushing between the wads of paper.
5. Use the weeds cut with a scythe or lawnmower in Step 1 to hold the newspaper in place.

If necessary, other mulching materials such as lawn mowings may be used to hold the paper down. Bean and pea netting held down at intervals with bricks could also be tried. If cardboard is available it can replace newspaper in the above method and is somewhat easier to use. Newspaper and cardboard mulches can be planted through in the same way as for the thin polythene described above.

It is difficult to say how long a mulch will take to destroy the weeds beneath it. The time taken will depend on the type of weeds present, whether or not the weeds were broken up with a mechanical cultivator before applying the mulch, and the time of year that the mulch was applied. Fine grasses such as those found in a lawn, chickweed and other annual weeds are quite easy to kill, but deep-rooted perennials such as docks and thistles are much more difficult. Obviously, those weeds which have large roots and a good store of food are much more resistant to starvation caused by light exclusion than are plants with small roots. The best method of getting rid of docks is to loosen the soil with a fork once the mulch has been removed, and then simply pull them out. Breaking up the weed roots with a mechanical cultivator prior to covering will reduce the food supply and make them die more quickly. Mulches applied in the summer, when weeds are growing strongly, will be more effective than those applied during the winter when plant growth slows down. Bearing in mind the above variables, it should take about six months for a light-excluding mulch to kill off most weeds. Even if there are a few left when the mulch is removed, the job of digging them out will be much easier than it would have been without the mulch.

When mulches are finally removed from an area that had been overgrown for a long time there will be massive germination of weed seeds. Provided that no crops are planted immediately, these weeds can easily be killed by hoeing.

Left:
. . . until the desired area is covered.

Above:
Hold the newspaper down with mowings.

Right:
This type of hoe is useful for dealing with large areas of weeds.

Far right:
Seed potato ready for planting.

EXAMPLE 2 — GROWING POTATOES UNDER A MULCH

If potato tubers are exposed to the light they become green and poisonous. The conventional way of preventing this happening consists of planting the seed potatoes fairly deeply and then earthing up the plants during the growing season. This method involves a fair amount of hard work and is obviously no good for use in a no-dig gardening system. No-dig methods of growing potatoes rely on placing the tubers on or near the soil surface and then covering them with a mulch to exclude the light. Organic mulches need to be applied fairly thickly to be lightproof and so quite a large amount of material will be required for the average gardener's potatoes. I first read about no-dig potatoes in the HDRA newsletter and they suggested using hay topped up with grass mowings during the season. This combination produces a dense mulch which is effective at stopping the light. The cost of the hay is one disadvantage, unless spoiled hay can be obtained, and there may also be trouble caused by weed seeds, brought in with the hay, which will germinate at a later date. Composted stable manure can be used as a mulch to grow potatoes, but has to be used in large quantities. The partly decomposed nature of the manure means that it is rapidly taken into the soil by earthworms and this leads to some of the potatoes becoming exposed and green. Many allotment sites have spare pieces of land which can provide a

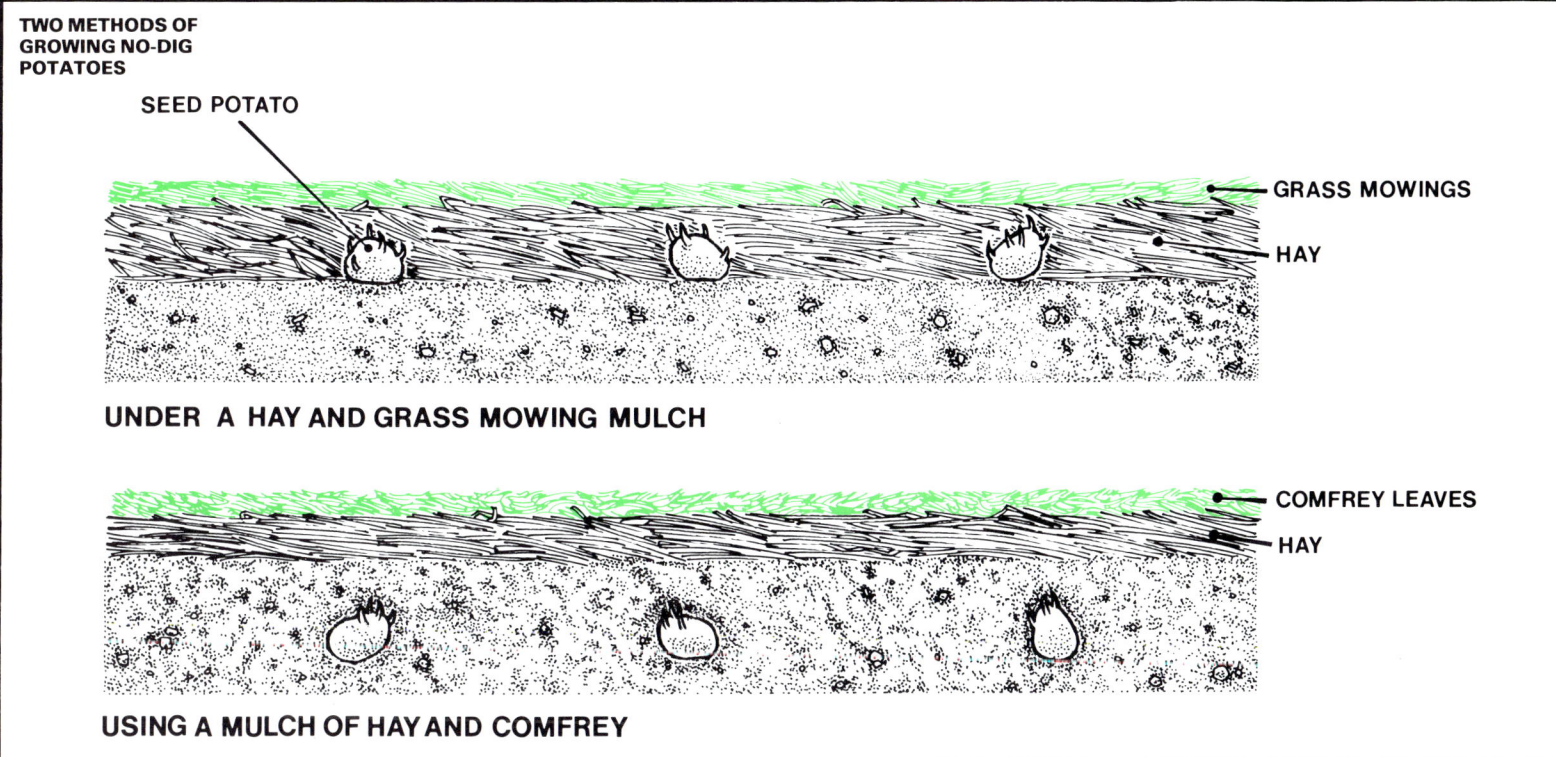

TWO METHODS OF GROWING NO-DIG POTATOES

SEED POTATO

GRASS MOWINGS

HAY

UNDER A HAY AND GRASS MOWING MULCH

COMFREY LEAVES

HAY

USING A MULCH OF HAY AND COMFREY

cut of hay early in the season before the weed seeds have set. For gardeners who find it impossible to bring in material to mulch their potatoes, the alternative is for them to grow their own. Comfrey can be used as a mulch but rots down rather too readily on its own and so is better combined with something more fibrous. Green manure crops such as grazing rye and alfalfa can be fitted into a gardening rotation and will provide some more lasting mulching material. Unless it is saved from the previous autumn, home-grown mulching material is unlikely to be available when seed potatoes are due to be planted. Planting the potatoes a couple of inches below the soil level with a trowel will overcome this difficulty. The potato shoots will take some time to break through the soil surface and by then sufficient mulching material should be available to protect the shoots from frost.

● **Growing No-dig Potatoes on a 4ft-Wide Bed**

1. Hoe through any weeds.
2. Using a trowel, plant seed potatoes 1ft apart each way and approximately 2in below the soil surface.
3. If available, apply a dressing of compost or rotted manure.
4. As soon as it becomes available, cover, first with some sort of hay, and then with comfrey leaves or lawn mowings.
5. As the season progresses, the mulch should be built up by pushing more material between the potato plants.
6. The mulch should be dense enough to suppress almost all weeds but any that do come up should be pulled out by hand.
7. The potato crop can be harvested by pulling off the potato tops, moving aside the mulch and perhaps a small amount of soil, and then simply picking the potatoes up.

In the above growing system, quite a lot of water will be absorbed by the mulch before any can reach the soil. This means that when watering it is better to apply a lot of water infrequently than it is to use little and often. The protective nature of the mulch means that buckets of water can be thrown on without damaging the soil surface and this can speed up watering on allotments where the use of a hose is not possible.

Some of the mulch will decompose during the growing season, especially if comfrey is used, and this will provide extra food for the potatoes.

Provided that the soil has not been dug for some time before the potatoes are planted, it should be firm enough to prevent the tubers going deep and requiring a fork to remove them.

Some people do not like growing potatoes under a mulch because of slug damage. In my garden however, slug damage to potatoes has become far less of a problem since they have been grown under a mulch than it was when they were grown conventionally. As usual in gardening, it is difficult to establish a direct relationship between cause and effect, but the improvement may be due to one or more of the following reasons. Frogs have been introduced into the garden and there is now quite a large population of them. As the mulches decay, they provide an alternative source of food for the slugs which they can eat instead of the potatoes. The mulch provides a good home for centipedes, devil's coach horses and other carnivorous animals and perhaps some of these help to keep down the slug population.

Growing potatoes by the above method leaves plenty of organic matter incorporated in the surface of the soil and this will be of great benefit to the next crop. Any remaining mulch may be either left where it is or removed to the compost heap, depending on how much it has decayed and on the requirements of the following crop.

Right:
The tubers have been planted just below the soil surface and a layer of 'hay' has been placed on the soil.

Left:
A layer of comfrey has now been added.

Below left:
The potato tops have grown through the mulch . . .

Right:
. . . and tubers are beginning to develop beneath it.

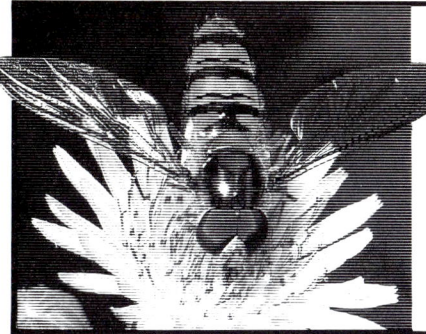

10 Pest and Disease Control

Below:
Ladybirds eat aphids . . .

Changing over to organic gardening means adopting a completely different approach to pest and disease control, and is not just a matter of exchanging chemical pesticides for organic alternatives. In many cases, pesticides are simply substituted for good husbandry, and I would not recommend using even organic sprays until other methods of control have failed. Accepting a small amount of damage to some crops will also reduce the need for spraying.

Organic Methods of Control

- Create a fertile soil
- Provide good growing conditions
- Do not destroy predators
- Rotate crops
- Use barriers
- Grow resistant varieties
- Time sowing to avoid attack
- Use biological control
- Spray with organic pesticides

As emphasised by the first four items in the list, pest and disease control should be part of a complete organic gardening system. Taking my own garden as an example, the only pesticide required is soap solution for occasional use against aphids. I will now give a detailed description of the above methods.

● Create a Fertile Soil
Chapters 4 and 7 covering 'Composting' and 'Green Manuring' have already provided information about how to achieve this aim, and all I need to do here is mention the connection with pest and disease control. Organic methods of supplying a plant

with its food should ensure a steady supply of nutrients resulting in strong, healthy growth. Feeding with soluble chemicals, on the other hand, can result in soft foliage which is prone to pest and disease attack. By providing a full range of plant foods, a fertile soil will also prevent deficiency diseases occurring.

● Provide Good Growing Conditions

If healthy plants are to be grown, it is necessary to provide them with as near to ideal conditions as possible. Following the advice given in other chapters of this book about avoiding waterlogging of the soil, correcting its pH and improving its structure with compost and manure will enable plants to develop a good root system. The technique of pre-germination can be used to protect seeds that rot easily, and providing warmth for the seedlings will keep them growing strongly. Greenhouses should be ventilated sufficiently to avoid the accumulation of stagnant air and subsequent disease.

● Do Not Destroy Predators

One of the disadvantages of pesticides is that they may not only kill the pest for which they are intended, but may also destroy beneficial creatures such as hoverflies. In this way, spraying can upset the natural balance and lead to even greater numbers of pests and more reliance on pesticides to keep them in check. It is possible for the gardener to go further than just sparing hoverflies — they can actually be attracted into the garden by growing certain plants on which they feed. Trials by the HDRA

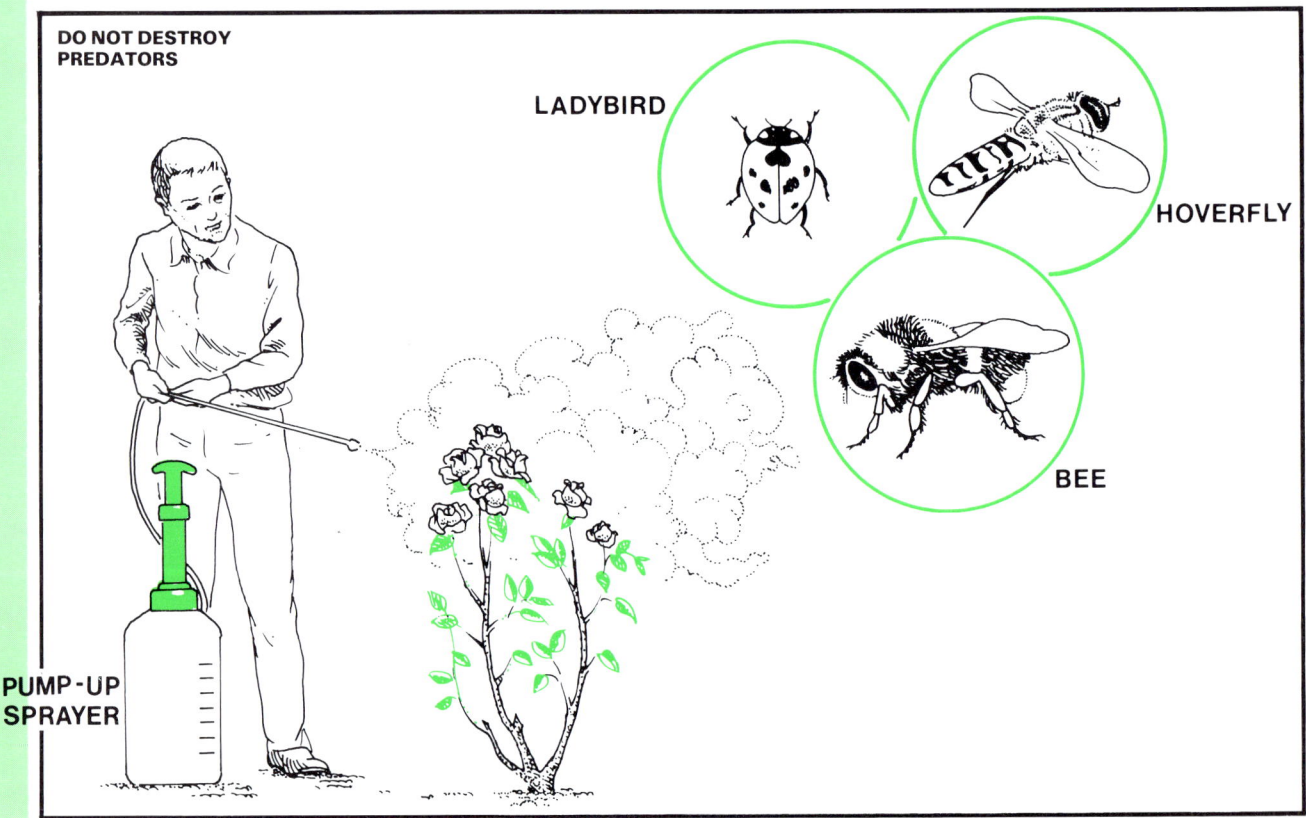

DO NOT DESTROY PREDATORS

LADYBIRD

HOVERFLY

BEE

PUMP-UP SPRAYER

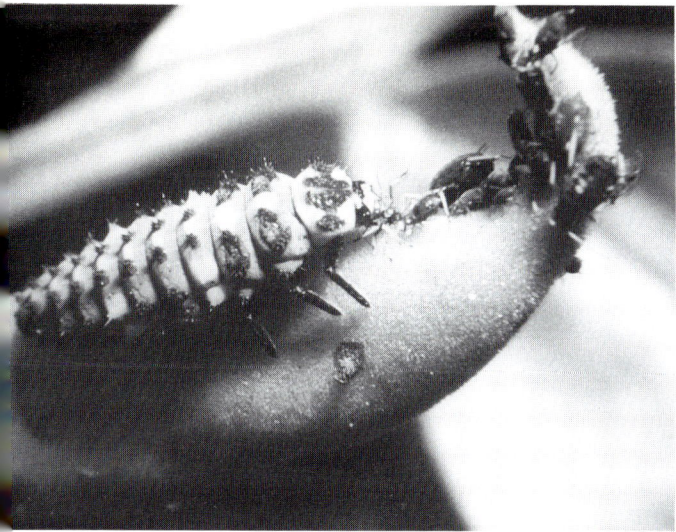

have shown *Limnanthes douglasii* (poached egg plant), *Convolvulus tricolour* and Buckwheat to be very good in this respect.

● Rotate Crops

Rotating the planting of vegetables around the garden instead of growing them in the same place every year has two main advantages. Firstly, nutrients are removed from the soil in an even manner. During the rotation, each piece of land will be used to grow both heavy feeding and light feeding crops and this will prevent depletion of the soil in one area. Secondly, the build-up of soil-borne pests and diseases will be reduced. For example, growing potatoes in a different section of the garden each year will lessen the chances of a serious eelworm attack.

When planning a vegetable garden, the first thing to do is divide up the land into four roughly equal sections. If a system of beds and paths is to be used, this may mean that one bed in each section will have to be narrower than the rest. The next step is to decide which crops are to be grown and what quantity of each is required. Personal taste must be taken into account because there is no point in growing unwanted vegetables. If plenty of space is available, green manures can be fitted into the rotation to improve soil fertility and increase the time before a particular crop returns to the same section. The most important point to remember is that each family of plants should only be grown once on the same section during a rotation cycle.

Above left:
. . . and so do their larvae!

Above:
Poached egg plants will help to attract . . .

Left:
. . . hoverflies to the garden.

Below:
Square of rubber underlay around brassica plant.

The following example shows the basic crop rotation in each section of my own garden.

Crop	Soil Treatment
Year 1 Potatoes Tomatoes	Manure applied in the spring, ground limestone applied once crops have been removed. Tomatoes undersown with alfalfa, early potatoes followed by grazing rye
Year 2 Brussels sprouts interplanted with Lettuce; Cabbages; Broad beans followed by Spring cabbages	Heavy application of compost

Crop	Soil Treatment
Year 3 Carrots Parsnips Beetroot Chard Onions	Carrots and parsnips not fed, other crops given compost
Year 4 Sweet corn Courgettes Pumpkins	Application of compost and/or manure as available

In case there is any confusion, the following diagram should help to clarify the matter. The four squares represent sections of the garden, and the crops move clockwise.

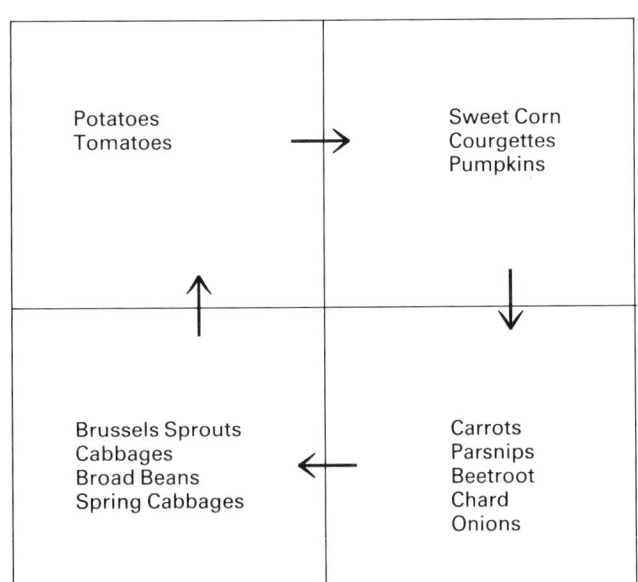

Potatoes
Tomatoes → Sweet Corn
Courgettes
Pumpkins ↓

Brussels Sprouts
Cabbages
Broad Beans
Spring Cabbages ← Carrots
Parsnips
Beetroot
Chard
Onions ↑

● **Use Barriers**

A number of pests can be prevented from damaging crops by putting a barrier in their way. Various forms of this technique can be used against a variety of pests and it has the advantage of not leaving poisonous residues.

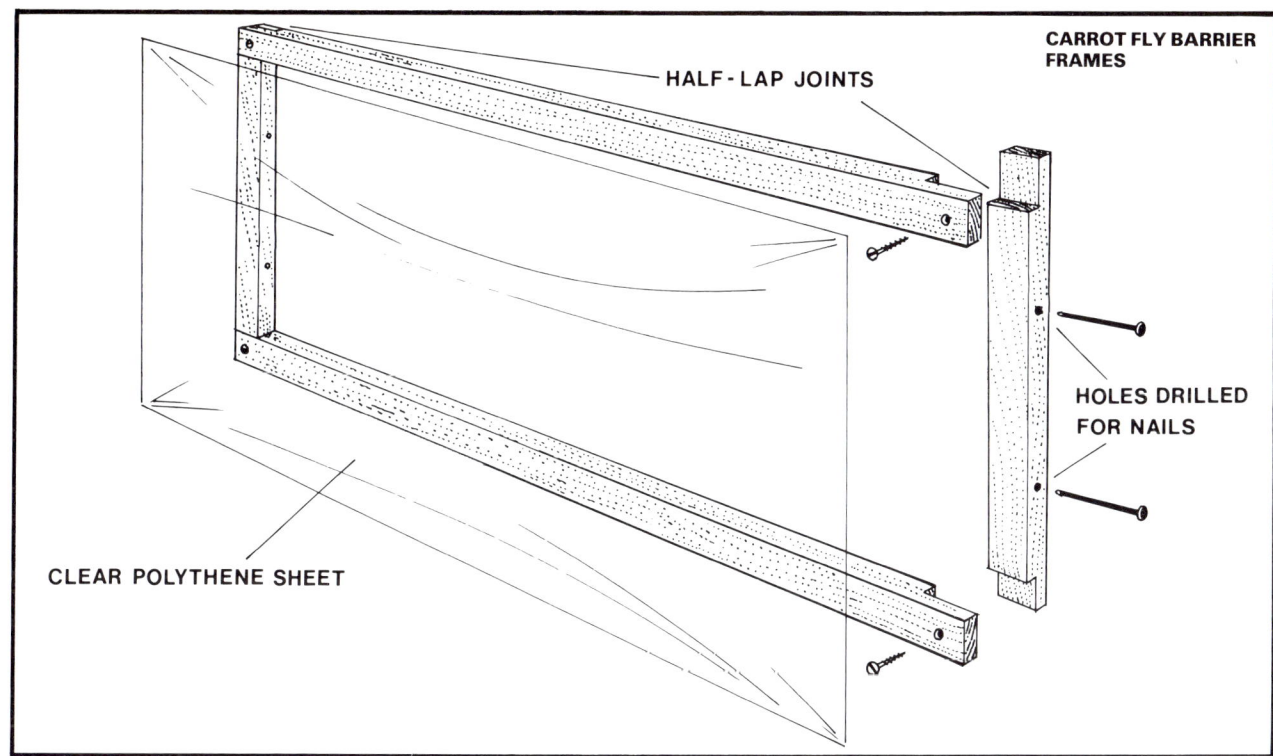

HALF-LAP JOINTS

CARROT FLY BARRIER FRAMES

HOLES DRILLED FOR NAILS

CLEAR POLYTHENE SHEET

Underlay Square

Cabbage root flies lay their eggs at the base of cabbage stems and the resulting maggots tunnel into the plants causing serious damage. The easiest way of avoiding such an attack is to prevent the flies laying their eggs by covering the soil around the plant with a 6in square of foam rubber carpet underlay. A small hole should be made in the centre of the square to accommodate the plant stem and a slit must be cut from this hole to the outside of the square so that it can be placed in position.

Polythene 'Fence'

The amount of damage done to carrots by carrot fly can be considerably reduced by erecting a protective barrier of polythene. The enclosure needs to be about 2ft high and must protect the carrots on all sides. My first attempt at making such a barrier was a dismal failure because I underestimated the effect

of strong winds on vertical sheets of polythene. I had used thin polythene supported by canes to erect the structure which lasted only a couple of hours. I have since built a number of wooden frames which are covered with thick polythene and can be fixed together to form enclosures of various sizes. The frames were made using half lap joints fixed with waterproof glue and galvanised screws. The polythene, which lasts a couple of years, is tacked in place with a staple gun. The frames have been drilled so that nails can be pushed through the holes to hold them together. Numbering of the frames ensures that the holes match when they are being put together.

As can be seen by the diagram, there is no covering over the top of the enclosure — its effectiveness relying on the low-flying nature of carrot flies. The use of this technique has reduced carrot fly damage in my garden to an acceptable level rather than eliminating it. Using a barrier of greater height would

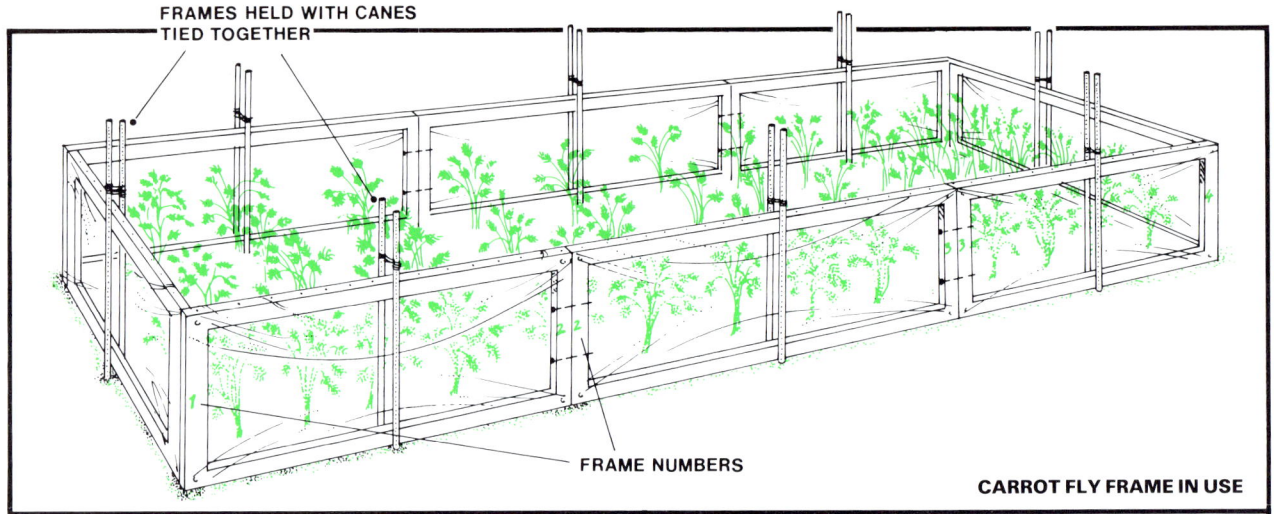

FRAMES HELD WITH CANES
TIED TOGETHER

FRAME NUMBERS

CARROT FLY FRAME IN USE

probably reduce the damage still further, but this would mean removing the structure to enable weeding and thinning to be carried out. The shelter from wind provided by the barrier results in higher temperatures and faster growth for the carrots. This effect is also used to advantage by erecting the frames around newly planted runner beans at a time when carrot fly protection is not required.

'Agryl' Fleece

I have been experimenting with this product for only a short time, but have been quite impressed. It is a very lightweight cloth made of polypropylene fibres which allows water and light to reach the plants over which it is placed. I have not been using the material for long enough to be able to judge its useful life, and so I find it difficult to comment on its value for money.

It is recommended that the cloth is laid over plants or seeds and held down by placing soil on its edges. I have also used the cloth to cover a home-made frame and grown cabbages underneath. Apart from protection against pests, 'Agryl' has the advantages of frost protection, shelter from wind, and extra warmth from its 'greenhouse' effect.

I would suggest trying 'Agryl' fleece as protection against the following pests: flea beetle, carrot fly, caterpillars (keeps off butterflies) and cabbage root fly.

Grease Bands

These are used on trees to prevent the upward movement of harmful insects. An alternative method of providing a similar barrier is to apply fruit tree grease around the trunk of the tree.

GREASE BAND ON FRUIT TREE

GREASE BAND

Far left:
The carrot fly barrier frames will also provide some protection for plants that are being hardened off . . .

Left:
. . . and for newly planted runner beans.

Right:
Lettuces grow under 'Agryl' fleece.

Below:
Hispi cabbages grown under 'Agryl'. A home-made support frame has been used in this case.

Below right:
Pigeons can do extensive damage to unprotected plants.

Netting
Fruit and vegetables that are attractive to birds can be protected with plastic netting. Specially made fruit cages are available for this purpose, but for small areas netting held in place by canes may be sufficient. The freshly cultivated soil of a seed bed is especially attractive to cats and these animals may also be kept off with netting.

● **Grow Resistant Varieties**
Some varieties of plants are much more resistant to pest and disease attack than others. Information about the relative resistance of various varieties can be found in seed and plant catalogues. Unfortunately, gaining an advantage in this respect may mean sacrificing other qualities such as flavour.

Greenhouse tomatoes are a difficult crop to rotate effectively because of the limited amount of space usually available under glass to the amateur grower. Growing in containers is one answer but this does require rather a lot of potting mixture. Another solution is to use grafted tomatoes and plant directly in the soil. KNVF rootstock is available from some seed merchants and will provide resistance to corky root, nematodes, *verticillium* and *fusarium*. The technique, which is not difficult, is fully described in the instructions sent out with the seeds.

● Time Sowing to Avoid Attack

A serious attack by blackfly on broad beans may result in the loss of the complete crop. One way of avoiding such an attack is to sow a hardy variety such as *Aquadulce Claudia* in the autumn. The plants will be ahead of spring-sown broad beans and this will allow the removal of the top 6in or so of the plants when the blackfly appear. The pest is therefore deprived of the young, soft growth and will find it much more difficult to attack the remaining, much tougher parts of the plants. After many years of success with autumn sowing of broad beans, I have now changed the technique somewhat because some of the plants may be lost during a severe winter. I now sow broad beans in containers in the greenhouse during January and plant them out during March. This method involves more effort than autumn sowing in the soil, but does avoid the losses due to the worst part of the winter.

Left:
A blackfly attack on broad beans.

FRUIT CAGE

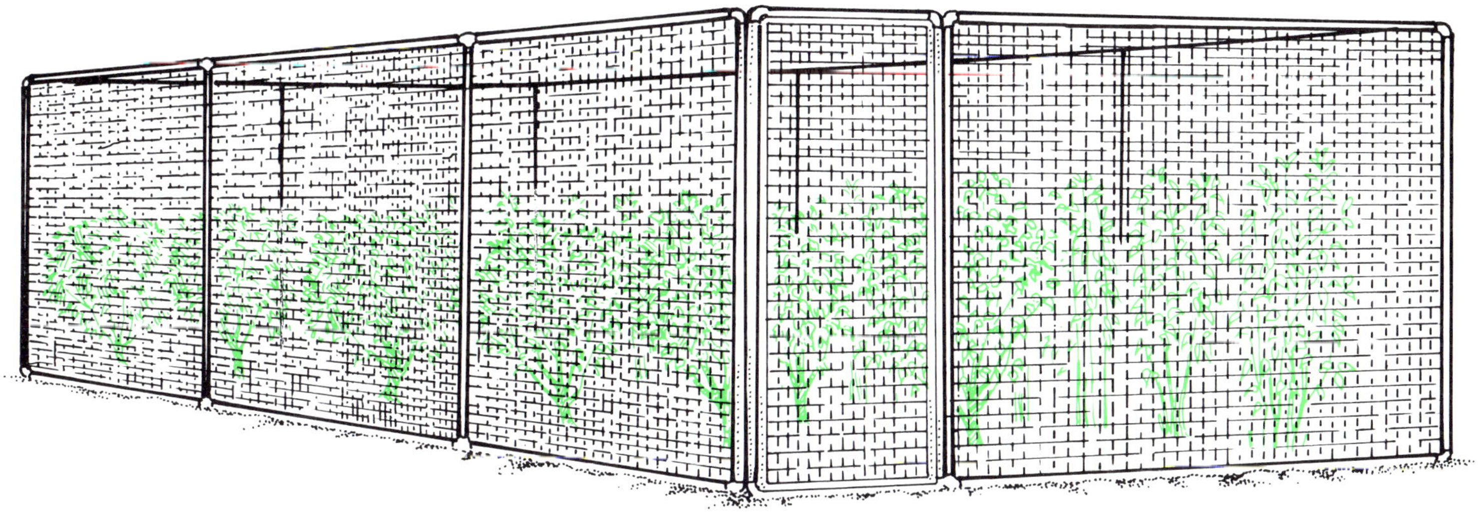

Above:
Broad beans sown in a 'Propapak' and raised under glass.

Right:
Bean and pea netting used horizontally will support and separate the plants as they grow.

Far right:
The early start given to the broad beans should ensure that they are well developed before blackfly appear.

● Use Biological Control

It is now possible for the amateur gardener to control several pests by using biological controls. The technique consists of purchasing a supply of the correct parasite or predator and then introducing it into the area where a pest attack is taking place.

Bacillus Thuringiensis

This is supplied in powder form and is mixed with water before being sprayed. Being specific to certain caterpillars, it is harmless to other forms of life. Cabbage caterpillars can be controlled very effectively by spraying *Bacillus Thuringiensis* on to the leaves which they are eating.

Glasshouse Whitefly Control

A whitefly attack on crops grown under glass can be controlled by introducing a tiny wasp called *Encarsia formosa*. This parasite is supplied on a leaf covered with infected whitefly larvae. The wasp should be introduced before the whitefly attack has become serious, but only if a temperature of at least 55°F can be maintained.

Red Spider Mite Control

This predator is called *Phytoseiulius persimilis* and is for use in greenhouses. The control will be more effective at higher temperatures, but can be started once the greenhouse has reached 55-60°F. The leaves on which the predators are dispatched should be cut up and placed on the plants being damaged by red spiders.

Trichoderma

Fruit trees suffering from silver leaf disease can be treated by drilling holes in the trunks and inserting pellets containing *Trichoderma*. A powder form of this substance is available for use against fungal attack on pruning cuts. The powder can either be mixed with water to form a paste and applied by brush, or be diluted further and then sprayed.

● Spray with Organic Pesticides

Bordeaux Mixture

This fungicide, made by mixing lime and copper sulphate, was originally used by French vine growers. It can be used as a protective spray against potato blight, peach leaf curl and other fungal diseases.

Derris

Supplied as either dust or liquid, this insecticide should be used with care because it kills fish and some beneficial insects. Derris is effective against caterpillars, aphids and flea beetle.

Pyrethrum

Like derris, pyrethrum is made from a plant and therefore does not build up in the environment. It is harmful to bees, ladybirds and some other beneficial insects, but does break down and become harmless soon after it is sprayed. Used against aphids, sawfly and flea beetles.

Left:
Remove the top few inches of growth to prevent a blackfly attack.

Quassia
This pesticide is supplied as chips of wood which have to be boiled to extract the active ingredients. It is harmless to bees and ladybirds and can be used to control small caterpillars, sawflies and aphids.

Soft Soap
This can be used as a wetting agent for other pesticides, or on its own to control aphids and whitefly.

Savona Insecticidal Soap
Supplied as a liquid concentrate, Savona should be diluted with soft water before being sprayed. Suitable for use against aphids, whitefly, spider mites and mealy bugs.

Vegetable Pests and Diseases

● Beans — Broad, French and Runner

As previously described, the best control of *Blackfly* on broad beans is autumn sowing and subsequent removal of soft growth in the spring. This pest can also cause trouble on runner beans by destroying the growing tips. To prevent the beans being set back in this way, the blackfly can be killed with soap solution.

When I first grew broad beans in my garden, some of the plants suffered from *Chocolate Spot*. This fungus disease produces dark brown spots on the plants and is related to a mineral deficiency. In my case, all that was needed to prevent the disease recurring was an increase in soil fertility.

Above:
Quassia chips have to be boiled in water to produce an insecticide.

Right:
Aphids can be controlled by spraying with soap.

● **Brassicas**

Plants in this group such as cabbages, brussels sprouts, turnips, swedes, etc are very popular with gardeners and also with pests. *Cabbage Mealy Aphids* can be controlled by spraying with soap solution or by knocking them off with a jet of water from a hose.

An attack by *Caterpillars* can be avoided by using a netting or 'Agryl' barrier to keep off the offending butterflies and prevent them laying eggs. Alternatively, spray with *Bacillus Thuringiensis*.

Squares of carpet underlay, described under the heading 'Barriers', are the answer to *Cabbage Root Fly*.

I use a powerful jet of water from a hose to knock the *Whiteflies* off my brussels sprouts plants and this controls their numbers sufficiently for me to get a good crop. Regular spraying with soap solution is another remedy.

Fortunately, *Clubroot* is a disease that I do not have in my garden or allotment. Once soil is infected with this disease, a crop rotation of four years is insufficient to wipe it out because the spores can lie dormant for many years. Accepting brassica plants as gifts from other gardeners is one way of introducing the disease into one's own garden and so this should be avoided. The best organic answer for gardeners who already have clubroot-infected soil is to grow brassicas in a 'V' trench. The plants should be grown to a good size in 4-5in pots, using uninfected potting mixture. A 'V' trench approximately 5in deep should then be made in the soil and the brassicas planted in the bottom. As the plants develop, fill the trench around them with 'clean' compost or potting mixture. Although the brassicas will still develop clubroot, they should also produce a worthwhile crop.

● **Carrots**

The control of *Carrot Fly* is described under the heading 'Barriers'.

● **Cucumbers**

Red Spider Mite can be controlled with the predator *Phytoseiulius persimilis* mentioned under 'Biological Controls'.

● **Peas**

The *Pea Moth* is responsible for the small caterpillars often found inside peas. Spraying with soft soap and quassia about a week after the peas have started to flower is the method of control recommended by the HDRA.

● **Potatoes**

There is no cure for *Potato Blight* but spraying with Bordeaux mixture is a preventative measure.

Crop rotation is the best defence against the build-up of *Potato Eelworm*. If this soil-borne pest is a problem, planting resistant varieties and growing potatoes on a no-dig system are methods of improving the yield.

Potato Scab is encouraged by a high soil pH and this is why lime should be kept away from potatoes in crop rotations. Manure and other forms of organic matter which increase soil acidity can be used to reduce the damage from this disease. I have found that growing potatoes on a no-dig system, using a mulch, produces potatoes almost free of scab.

Slugs may eat holes in potato tubers and cause damage to other types of vegetables, especially at the seedling stage. There are a number of ways in which the organic gardener can deal with slugs which include collecting them at night with the aid of a torch, catching them in various types of traps, keeping them away from plants with barriers and killing them with Fertosan Slug Killer. Judging by the number of people who are still looking for an answer to their slug problem, none of these solutions is really effective. I suggest that anyone troubled by slugs should build a pond and introduce frogs. Slugs and snails form a considerable part of a frog's diet and only a small pond is required for the purpose of raising tadpoles. Even if the frogs do not have a significant effect on the slug population, they will still be an interesting feature of the garden.

● **Tomatoes**

Greenhouse tomatoes can suffer considerable damage from an attack by *Whiteflies*, but this pest can be controlled by introducing *Encarsia formosa*. Another method of control that can be tried is the growing of tagetes plants among the tomatoes.

Grafted tomato plants, referred to under the heading 'Resistant Varieties', are a defence against *Soil-Borne Diseases*.

Below:
If you have trouble with slugs . . .

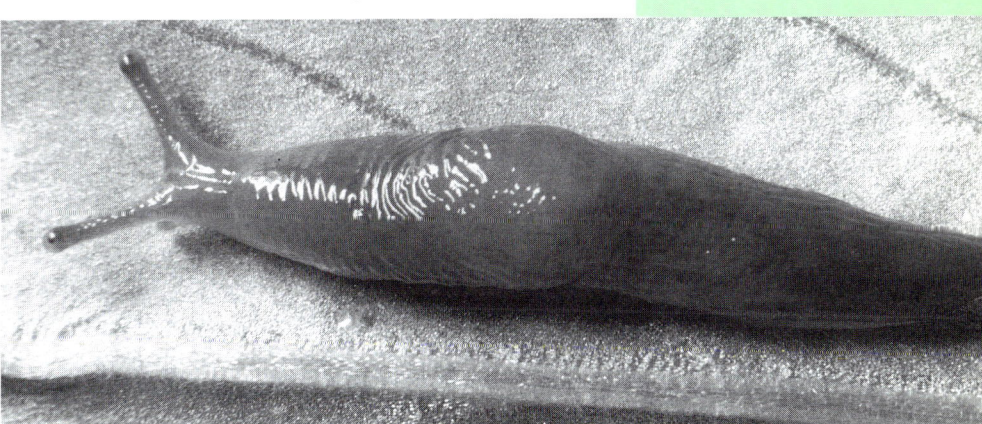

Fruit Pests and Diseases

● Aphids
Spray with soap solution or soap/quassia.

● Apple Sawfly
This pest feeds on developing fruitlets and can be controlled by spraying with derris within one week of petal fall.

● American Gooseberry Mildew
This appears as white powdery patches on shoots, leaves and berries. Control is a matter of avoiding overfeeding the bushes with nitrogen, pruning to keep the bushes 'open' and spraying with a solution of 1lb of washing soda and 4oz of soft soap dissolved in 5 gal of water.

● Black Currant Gall Mite
This pest is responsible for the 'big buds' seen on blackcurrants. Removal of enlarged buds in the winter and spraying the mites with soap/quassia when they hatch in the spring are the recommended controls.

● Codling Moth
The caterpillars of this moth cause 'maggoty' apples. Bands of sacking tied around the trees in the summer will trap caterpillars trying to climb up the trunks, and further control is a matter of destroying any apples that are seen to contain maggots.

● Gooseberry Sawfly
These green and black caterpillars can completely defoliate a bush in a very short time. The caterpillars can be controlled with derris.

● Peach Leaf Curl
This disease causes leaves to become crinkled with red and yellow discoloration. Keeping rain off the leaves during spring will prevent an attack of leaf curl and this can be achieved on fan-trained peaches by erecting a polythene shelter. Trees grown in pots can be moved into a greenhouse during the vulnerable time. Spraying with Bordeaux mixture will protect trees which cannot be kept dry.

● Silverleaf Disease
Pellets of *Trichoderma viride* described under the heading 'Biological Controls' can be used to treat this disease which mainly attacks plum trees.

I have only devoted a relatively small amount of space to specific remedies for pests and diseases so that the subject does not get out of proportion with the rest of the book. It is of particular concern to me that I do not give the impression that organic gardeners should be using the above pesticides as a matter of routine. I would suggest that anyone who has to use regular spraying as a control against a large variety of pests should look for ways to improve their basic organic gardening techniques.

Much more detailed information about the identification and control of pests and diseases can be found in two booklets published by the HDRA and entitled *Vegetable Pest and Disease Control* and *Fruit Pest and Disease Control the Organic Way*.

11 Potting Mixtures

The term 'Compost' is usually used to describe two different materials in gardening and this may lead to some confusion. In this book, 'Compost' refers to partly decomposed vegetable matter, and mixtures of soil, peat etc used for potting up are referred to as 'Potting Mixtures'.

There are a number of reasons why soil taken straight from the garden is less than ideal for use as a seed-sowing and potting medium.

Disadvantages of Plain Garden Soil as a Potting Medium

● **Weed Seeds**
The germination of weed seeds is of particular concern in seed-sowing mixtures where picking out the weeds from among plant seedlings can be rather time consuming.

● **Diseases**
Diseases carried in the soil may cause damage to the plants, eg damping off of seedlings.

● **Poor Structure**
Plants in pots tend to be watered more often than those grown directly in the ground and this can lead to breakdown of the soil structure causing poor drainage and damage to roots.

● **Insufficient Plant Foods**
Being restricted by the size of a container, the roots of a potted plant cannot explore a large volume of soil in search of food. Plants that require a high level of nutrients or are in a pot for a long time may therefore run short of food.

John Innes seed and potting mixtures were formulated to overcome these disadvantages. They are based on the use of soil but with the addition of peat, coarse sand or grit, fertilisers and chalk. These seed and potting mixtures are freely available from gardening shops and have the following advantages over plain garden soil.

● **Freedom from Weed Seeds and Diseases**
The soil component of John Innes mixtures is steam sterilised to kill seeds and plant diseases.

● **Good Structure**
Drainage is provided by the use of sand or grit, and peat helps to improve the moisture-holding capability of the mixtures.

● **High Level of Nutrients**
Added fertilisers provide extra plant foods and the amount can be adjusted according to the requirements of particular plants.

The quality of John Innes mixtures is dependent upon the variable nature of the soil from which they are made. This variability has led to the production of soilless potting mixtures. Usually, these are based on peat or a peat/perlite mix, with chemicals added to provide plant foods.

The chemicals used in both of the above types of commercially available potting mixtures make them unsuitable for organic gardeners. Organically-based mixtures are now available, but most gardeners should not find too much difficulty in making their own. Worm compost and comfrey peat have already been described in previous chapters and these materials can be used to provide the necessary plant foods. Although unsterilised soil does have disadvantages, I still like to include it in my potting mixtures. I find that with soil in the mixture, over- or under-watering is less likely, and the plants seem more eager to root into the surrounding soil when planted out, than do those of plants grown in soilless mixtures. Sterilisation of soil is not a particularly easy task for the average person to carry out, but I find that soil straight from the garden gives satisfactory results in most cases. I deal with any weeds that appear by simply pulling them out, and use the technique of pre-germination (explained later) to prevent certain seeds from rotting.

The way in which different gardeners carry out seed sowing and potting up varies considerably, eg the amount of pressure used to compact the potting mixture in a container. When the variable nature of materials such as comfrey peat and worm compost are also taken into account, it becomes obvious that I cannot give a formula for a universally ideal potting mixture. However, the following information should enable the gardener to get satisfactory results straight away, and then to make beneficial adjustments to the proportions after a few experiments. All proportions are by volume.

● **Mix No 1**
3 parts worm compost
3 parts sedge peat
1 part perlite

● **Mix No 2**
3 parts soil
2 parts worm compost
1 part sedge peat
1 part perlite

● **Mix No 3**
3 parts soil
2 parts comfrey peat
1 part sedge peat
1 part perlite

If calcified seaweed or ground limestone has not been used during the production of worm compost or comfrey peat, it may be necessary to add one of these materials to the above mixtures to raise the pH. A check could be done with a pH testing kit, but this is something I have never done as I always use calcified seaweed when making worm compost and comfrey peat.

Seed-sowing mixtures do not need such a high level of nutrients as do potting mixtures, and so only half the amount of worm compost or comfrey peat should be used.

Perlite is used to provide drainage in the above mixtures but could be substituted with an equal quantity of grit. Recently, I have been using potting mixtures containing neither of these drainage materials and the results make me wonder whether their inclusion is really necessary for most plants. I would still

advocate using perlite to produce free-draining mixtures for delicate seedlings, but I think it is worth experimenting to see if it can be omitted most of the time. Apart from taking care when watering, there are a couple of other things that can be done to ensure that potted plants do not become waterlogged. Firstly, the initial drainage will be improved if the potting mixture is not rammed hard into the container. Watering will eventually cause the mixture to sink, but by this time plant roots should be well into the fresh soil. Secondly, plants should not be moved on into too large a pot because this will leave a lot of potting mixture unexplored by plant roots. In my experience, drainage is not a problem once a plant has established an extensive root system within a pot.

Seed Sowing and Planting in Containers

The difficulties described in the first part of this chapter may have made the reader wonder why anyone bothers to sow seeds in containers instead of sowing them directly into the ground. My answer is that once a reliable formula is worked out, potting mixtures are not difficult to make, and that there are distinct advantages to be gained by growing some plants in pots before planting them out.

Below:
A garden frame can be used for raising plants from seed.

Far right:
PLANTING OUT LETTUCES: a divided tray of plants.

● Advantages

An Early Start

An early start to the season can be made if plants are raised in a greenhouse or cold frame and then planted outside once the weather has warmed up.

Better Germination

The greater control over factors such as temperature, given by sowing in seed trays instead of in the ground, should result in a higher proportion of seeds germinating.

Less Damage by Insects

As an example, raising my brassica plants under glass means that I avoid the flea beetles which attack seedlings in the open.

Less Trouble with Weeds

Plants grown in pots and then transplanted are easier to weed around than are directly-sown seedlings.

As far as disadvantages are concerned, sowing in containers takes more time, requires space in a greenhouse, and may result in a transplanting shock caused by root disturbance.

Left:
The location of the next planting hole is found with a measuring stick.

Below left:
A bulb planter is pushed into the ground and a plug of soil is removed.

94

Right:
A lettuce plant is placed in the hole . . .

Below right:
. . . and firmed into position.

● Types of Containers

Seed Trays

Available in full, half and quarter sizes, these plastic trays are suitable for seed sowing and potting. It is now possible to purchase tray dividers which will keep the roots of individual plants separate.

Divided Polystyrene Trays (Propapaks)

These can be filled with potting mixture much more quickly than could the equivalent number of separate pots and I have found them to be very useful. Expanded polystyrene is not the strongest of materials but the trays do last quite a long time if treated carefully.

Square Plastic Pots

I use these thin, inexpensive pots for plants that require more potting mixture than is held in one compartment of a 'Propapak', or when I have only a few plants to pot up.

Round Plastic Pots

These are of rigid construction, available in large sizes and usually used for plants that are kept permanently in a pot.

Biodegradable Pots

These pots are not removed from plants before they are put in the soil, and this is supposed to prevent root disturbance.

Above:
Brassica plants in a seed tray that has been fitted with plastic dividers.

Left:
Tomato seedlings in a quarter-size seed tray.

Obviously, the pots are only used once and this has to be taken into account when comparing their price with other types. The material used to make these pots has to be something of a compromise because it must not rot too fast and release the potting mixture prematurely, nor must it decay too slowly and prevent plant roots growing into the soil. I have tried a couple of types myself and I see no reason to recommend them to anyone else. The plants that I grew in the pots suffered severe root restriction and I do not normally have any difficulty when transplanting from plastic pots anyway.

Soil Blocks

The expense of buying containers can be avoided by making blocks of potting mixture. A tool is used to compress the mixture into shape and also makes a hole for seed sowing. The two main problems that I found when using this method were breaking up of the blocks during watering, and excessive drying of the potting mixture due to the lack of a surrounding pot.

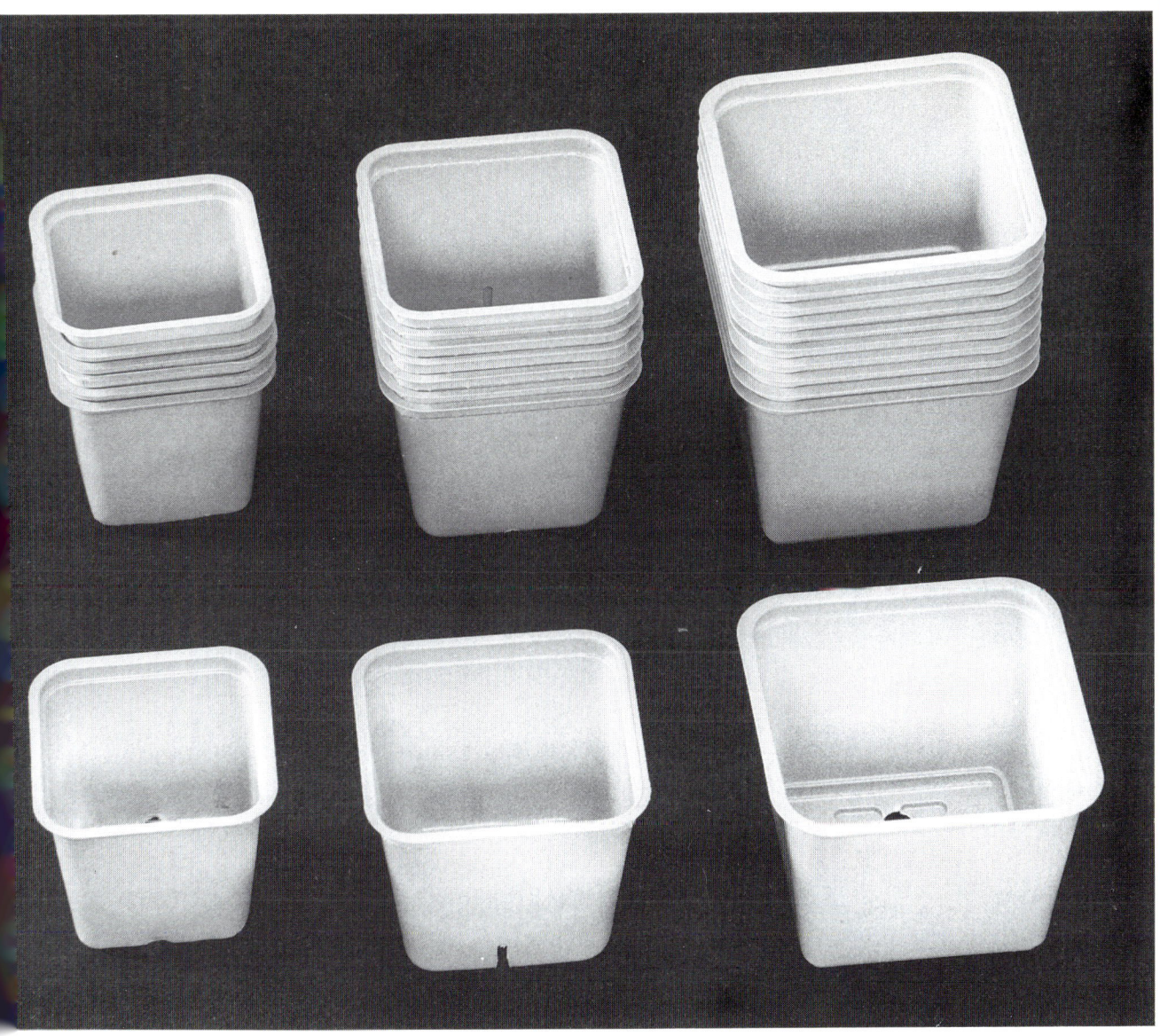

Above:
Pot plants are usually sold in rigid plastic pots.

Right:
Multiple-sown onions planted out.

● Fluid Sowing

This technique allows seeds to be sown in the open at an earlier date than would normally be possible. The seeds are germinated on damp tissue in a plastic sandwich box or similar container and kept in a warm place. Once roots begin to appear, the seeds are washed off the tissue into a kitchen sieve. The next step is to mix up some wallpaper paste and stir in the seeds. The paste must be of a type that does not contain fungicide and should be mixed to about three-quarters normal strength. A cake icing syringe or plastic bag with a corner cut off is then used to squeeze the seeds/gel mix into a seed drill. Care must be taken to prevent the soil drying out before the seedlings become established.

● Seed Sowing

I sow most of my seeds in trays of sieved potting mixture and then move the seedlings on into 'Propapaks' or plastic pots once they are large enough to handle. Some seeds do not germinate easily and may rot if conditions are unfavourable after sowing. Provided that they are large enough to make the procedure practicable, I pre-germinate such seed on damp tissue paper. As an example, I spread out my sweet corn seed in a tray lined with wet tissue and then place the tray in a polythene bag. Keeping the sweet corn in a warm place promotes rapid germination and the almost sterile conditions prevent the seeds rotting. Once the seeds split and roots appear, I move them into plastic pots of potting mixture. This technique also ensures that only viable seeds are sown.

● Multiple Sowing

Early crops of vegetables such as beetroot and onions can be grown by sowing in 'Propapaks' under glass and planting out later into warm soil. Growing one plant per compartment would be a very tedious business, but raising the number to four (multiple sowing) makes the technique feasible. If carrots are to be grown in this way, a stump-rooted variety should be chosen to avoid forking.

Left:
**Pregerminated sweet corn
seeds.**

12
My Own Garden

In the previous chapters I have tried to describe the various techniques of organic gardening, giving more than one method wherever possible. Local conditions such as soil type, weather, availability of manure and soil drainage combined with the personal preferences of the individual gardener, should determine which of these methods is chosen. The following description of my own garden is given as an example of a complete organic system.

When I took over the garden, about 16 years ago, it had not been cultivated for some time and was overgrown with couch grass. It took me some time to bring the whole garden back into cultivation, and I have modified the layout over the years. The soil is a fairly heavy loam to a depth of about 18in with a subsoil mixture of clay and gravel. Sufficient soil drainage throughout the garden means that waterlogging is not a problem. Trees and hedges in other gardens provide a fair amount of shelter from the wind.

Ornamental Garden

Originally, the garden shed used to be situated a few feet from the back of the bungalow. This provided easy access to tools etc, but obstructed the view from the kitchen window. Moving the shed to its present position, where it is camouflaged by the trellis and climbing plants, has permitted an unobstructed view of the ornamental garden. At one time, I did have a small lawn but this no longer exists now that the garden is laid out in its present form. My priorities of growing vegetables and having a pond mean that there would be little space left for a lawn and I do not consider that small areas of grass are worth the time spent on maintenance. The pond, with its surrounding shrubs and flowers, takes far less time to maintain than a properly cared-for lawn and its ever-changing nature makes it more interesting.

The fencing on either side of the ornamental garden is composed of slotted concrete posts and wooden panels. The concrete posts were spaced wide enough apart to enable easy removal of the fencing panels for subsequent treatment with wood preservative. Direct contact with the soil causes wooden fencing panels to decay and this has been avoided by concreting between the posts to above ground level. As shown in the diagram, wooden boards were clamped to the fencing posts at the desired height and the gap between the boards was filled with concrete. Provided that the slots in the fencing posts are long enough, ready-made concrete gravel boards can be used instead of the above method. Plastic bean and pea netting has now been attached to the fence to allow climbers such as sweet peas to be grown.

Conifers, rhododendrons and shrubs form the main framework of the ornamental garden, ensuring that it looks good throughout the year. Another advantage of having these plants is that they require very little attention once established. Extra colour is provided during the spring and summer months by planting various annuals between the conifers and shrubs. Interplanting with annuals in this manner has the advantage that the number used can be adjusted to suit the space left between the perennials as they grow larger. I usually grow three or four different types of annuals each year but restrict my choice to the smaller varieties. These compact plants are chosen so that they will not overcrowd the conifers and cause damage to them.

Woven black polypropylene has been fixed to the back of the trellis so that it is not possible to see the shed through the gaps in the climbing plants. I have found that the *Clematis montana*

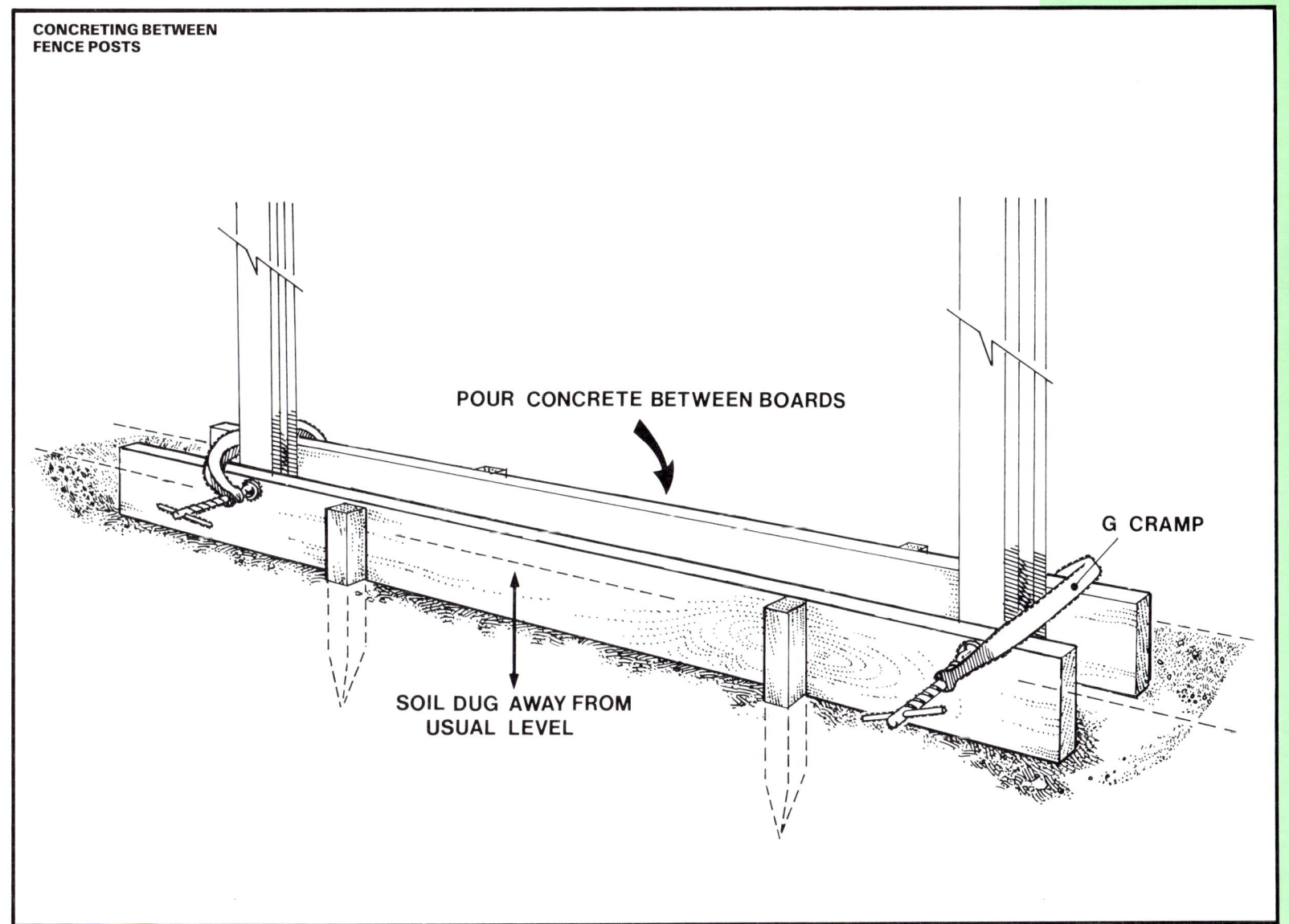

POUR CONCRETE BETWEEN BOARDS

G CRAMP

SOIL DUG AWAY FROM
USUAL LEVEL

Above:
Rhododendrons can be used to provide spring colour and a framework for a garden.

Right:
Juniperus communis **'Compressa' is a very small conifer suitable for planting in rock gardens.**

does not grow very well along the bottom of the trellis but have now filled this gap using variegated ivies.

As shown in the photograph, the ornamental garden area was completely cleared of perennial weeds before starting construction of the pond and planting of trees and shrubs. Any weeds that have appeared since, either from seeds already present in the soil or from those that have blown in from elsewhere, have been dealt with by the use of a hoe. During the growing season, all that is now necessary to keep the area weed-free is a couple of hours' work every few weeks. Rhododendrons and azaleas are grouped in one area of the garden where soil conditions have been made suitable for them. Before planting was carried out, sphagnum moss peat was incorporated into the top 6in of soil in this area to increase its acidity. Moss peat has also been applied to the soil surface of the rest of the ornamental garden, where its fibrous nature helps to improve the texture of the soil. The peat is applied to the soil surface and becomes mixed with the top inch or so of soil during hoeing. This treatment makes the soil resistant to compaction by treading and the effect is lasting because the peat does not readily break down.

Above left:
Iceland poppies are a particular favourite of mine.

Below left:
Pansies are so well known that they need no description.

Left:
Clematis Nellie Moser **is one of the climbing plants used to cover the trellis, along with** Clematis montana **and variegated ivies.**

Right:
The soil in the ornamental garden was cleared of weeds and levelled.

Below:
The ornamental garden in early summer 1987 . . .

Below right:
. . . and later the same year — from a different angle.

The soil fertility is maintained by occasional dressings of seaweed meal and well rotted manure. The seaweed is scattered on the soil surface at a rate of 4oz/sq yd every other autumn. As only a small amount of manure is required for this part of the garden, it is not easy to scatter it evenly and tidily even when well rotted. To overcome this problem, the manure is first processed by worm composting. I use an unmodified plastic dustbin as a container for this purpose and fill it with alternate layers of manure that has been composted as described in a previous chapter, and moss peat. The mixture, which is composed of approximately two parts manure to one of peat, usually contains sufficient manure worms and eggs for worm composting to begin, but more could be added from a worm bin if necessary. After about three weeks I tip out the contents of the bin to ensure thorough mixing and then return it to allow the worms to carry on their work. The worm compost is ready for use about two months after the processing began, and by this time it is very well broken down. I make use of the finished material by scattering it on the ornamental garden as if it were a granular fertiliser.

Left:
Its compact growing habit and attractive flowers make this miniature lilac a very desirable shrub.

Below:
The long flowering period of Geranium cinerium **makes it worthy of a place in the garden.**

Pond

In more than one sense of the word, a pond puts life into a garden. Wild creatures such as dragonflies and damsel flies will be attracted and can be supplemented by introducing fish and decorative plants. Moving water will make the pond even more interesting and this can be provided by using a pump to supply a waterfall or fountain.

Before starting work on the construction of my pond, I spent some time weighing up the pros and cons of the various materials available. In my opinion, concrete has two main advantages. Firstly, it provides a very firm foundation to which edging stones may be fixed and, secondly, it has a natural appearance without the folds commonly associated with liners. Concrete does have a number of disadvantages however, and these should be considered by anyone thinking of using it to construct a pond. It is hard work mixing and laying the concrete, the concrete may crack if thick ice is allowed to form during the winter, and if leaking does occur it is difficult to make an effective repair.

An irregular oval fairly describes the shape of my pond and this was chosen in preference to a more formal rectangle. During the construction of a rectangular pond, wooden shuttering is normally used to retain the concrete while it sets but this is impractical on a pond with curved sides.

Below:
Dragonfly larva underwater.

Right:
Newly emerged adult dragonfly.

The ground was levelled off and the rough shape of the pond was marked out using a hosepipe before excavation began. Digging out the top soil was a relatively easy task but the real difficulty began when I reached the subsoil. Eventually, I had to resort to using a pickaxe to loosen the mixture of clay and gravel before I could shovel it out. Fortunately, the sloping sides did mean that the area to be dug diminished as I went deeper. The finished pond is 2ft at its deepest but the depth of the hole had to be made greater than this to allow for the thickness of the concrete base and the sunken design of the pond. The hole was therefore dug out to a depth of about 3ft 6in below the level of the surrounding garden. To ensure that the sides of the hole would be firm and not prone to crumbling, the soil had been well trodden down before digging commenced and the completed hole was plastered with clay. The hole was then lined with a polythene sheet to prevent any chance of contamination of the concrete with soil during construction.

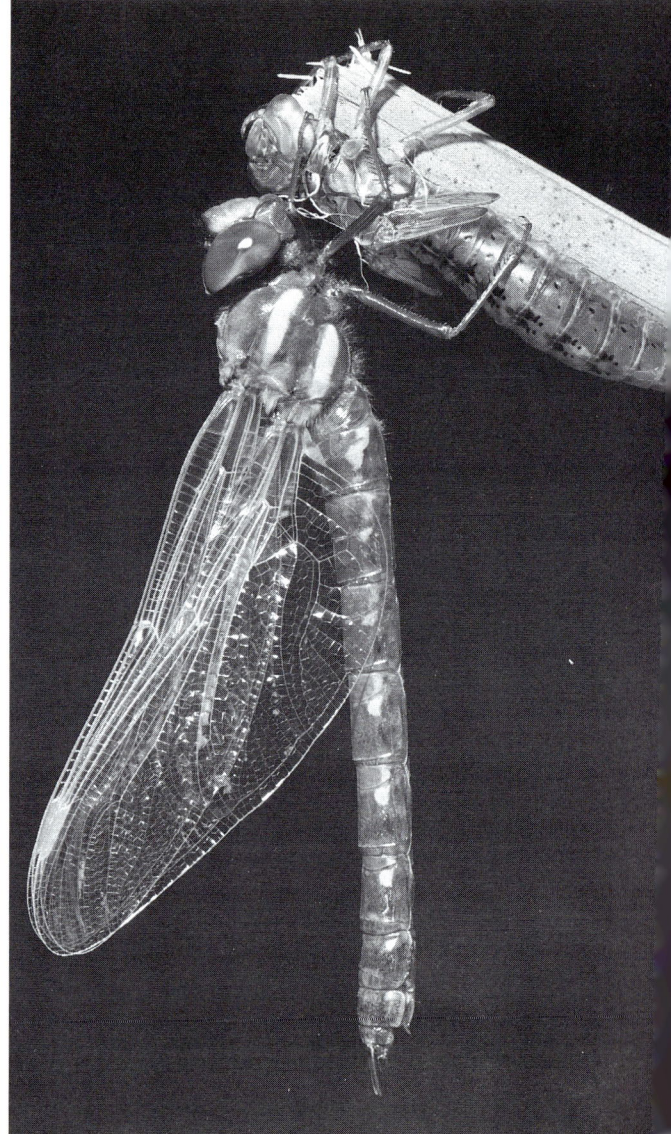

As previously mentioned, cracking can be a problem with this type of pond, and I therefore decided to reinforce the concrete with steel. The material used for this purpose was galvanised steel wire in the form of a 2in square mesh which was obtained from a garden centre. A reinforcing cage was made up in the shape of the pond by cutting and then wiring together pieces of the mesh. To be effective, the steel reinforcement needs to be embedded in concrete and so temporary spacers were used to keep it away from the sides of the hole while the concrete was being laid. These spacers were made by cutting plastic roofing sheet into widths of one corrugation.

Before actually starting to lay the concrete, I decided to erect a temporary polythene shelter over the hole as a precaution against rain. Having the pond filling up with water during construction was not a pleasant thought! As it happened, the weather was fine and the shelter was adapted to provide shade for the concrete from the hot sun. I concreted the base of the pond the evening before the main construction was to begin so that it would be firm enough to stand on and complete the work the next day. It was necessary to mix approximately one yard of ballast with the appropriate amount of cement and water to construct the pond, and I was fortunate enough to have the assistance of my wife and a couple of friends and the use of a concrete mixer to help me with this task. Thorough mixing of the materials was much easier using the mixer than it would have been by hand.

To prevent rapid changes of temperature occurring, the volume of water in a pond should be large in comparison to its surface area. To fulfil this requirement, the sides of my pond had to be made steep and this, combined with the lack of shuttering, caused the concrete to slide downwards as it was being laid. This difficulty was overcome by building the concrete up to a height of only a few inches and then working around the pond until the starting point was reached. By this time, the original concrete was slightly firmer and another layer could be added. As the process continued, trapping the reinforcing mesh, the plastic spacers were withdrawn. The wall thickness produced was approximately 4in and the top of the pond was finally reached. Next, a polythene sheet was placed over the pond to prevent evaporation of water from the concrete.

A few hours later, when the concrete had become firm, I used a trowel to apply a ½in thick rendering coat of sand and cement. This mixture was composed of three parts sharp sand, one part cement and the appropriate amount of waterproofing powder. The polythene was then put back on. During the next couple of days, a combination of spraying with water and covering with the polythene ensured that the concrete did not dry out. Pieces of hardboard were then wedged into position in the pond and

Above:
Westmorland rock can be obtained from many garden centres.

Left:
Fish do tend to become excited when they are fed.

emptying the pond and killing the fish if failure of the pipe to the upper pond should occur. Particles of sludge tend to settle out of the water as it passes through the upper pond to form a thick black layer on the bottom. Occasionally, I pump out the top pond to remove this sludge. It has never been necessary to empty the bottom pond completely but I do pump out some of the water and replace it with fresh every now and then.

I introduced frog spawn into the garden some years ago and there is now a thriving colony of frogs present. Frog spawn was obtained from a friend's pond which is a better idea than taking it from the wild. Large frogs seem to live quite happily with the fish in my large pond, but I remove any spawn that they lay there and place it in the upper pond. A piece of fine plastic netting of the type used for greenhouse shading is fixed across the mouth of the upper pond to prevent tadpoles going over the waterfall to provide a meal for the fish below.

During the coldest part of the winter, a 1in thick raft of polystyrene is floated on the large pond. This was made from polystyrene slabs bought from a builder's merchant and it covers a large area of the pond. The insulation provided by this raft considerably reduces the heat loss from the water and therefore makes it far less likely that the pond will freeze right over.

Vegetable Garden

My main interest in gardening is growing vegetables and so this part of the garden tends to be used for a number of experiments. Although I have insufficient space for carrying out a large number of tests, I do try to conduct some experiments each year. Another factor which limits the amount of testing that I can do is the incidence of pest and disease attack in my garden. For instance, my soil is not infected with clubroot and I have no intention of bringing in the disease just to do experiments. The results of tests carried out in one garden, for a single year, have to be treated with some caution. The apparent benefits produced by a particular growing technique may not be repeated in following years or in other gardens. The HDRA has a great advantage in this respect because its members have gardens throughout the country and this enables techniques to be evaluated under various conditions.

About five years ago, I set up a system of beds and paths in my garden as described in Chapter 3. Since then I have followed a policy of no-digging. Manure and compost are applied to the soil surface and I rely on hoeing and the action of earthworms to incorporate these materials.

I sow most of my seeds in trays or 'Propapaks' and raise the plants in a heated frame or greenhouse. This gives me control

the concrete shelves were cast in place. Sufficient time was given for these shelves to harden and then the pond was filled with water to see whether it leaked. Fortunately, it did not. The small upper pond was constructed by the method described above.

The next job was to fix edging stones made of Westmorland rock around the edges of the ponds using a sharp sand and cement mortar. Overflow holes for the pond were provided by pushing a steel rod through this mortar in a couple of places before it had set. A gap was left under one of the large stones so that frogs could get in and out of the pond and another, smaller, gap was left to accommodate the hose from the pump. Both ponds were treated with a proprietary compound to neutralise the lime content of the cement before stocking with plants and fish.

I use a submersible pump to power the waterfall and this is run continuously. Pumps vary in their efficiency and the model that I chose, although expensive to buy, has proved relatively cheap to run because the power it consumes is low compared to its water output. The pump is positioned at about shelf level in the pond rather than on the bottom, to avoid the possibility of over growing conditions and provides an early start to the season. Once these plants have been removed, tomatoes, cucumbers etc are grown under glass. I must say that I have not yet worked out a way to use the greenhouse space efficiently during the winter.

The crop rotation system in my garden is slightly unusual, mainly because I do not usually grow peas. It is normally recommended that potatoes should be followed by legumes but, as I do not wish to fill a whole section of the garden with broad beans, I put brassicas into this part of the rotation as well. Root vegetables, such as carrots, are grown as the third part of the rotation and this leaves the fourth year for sweet corn and courgettes. On my allotment, where cultivation is far from intensive, I omit root crops from the system. This allows me to fit in a green manure crop of clover prior to potatoes and still retain a four-year rotation. Obviously, this would not be a suitable rotation for allotment holders who do not have a garden in which to grow their carrots etc.

A few years ago I decided to remove the privet hedge which acted as a fence on one side of my garden and replace it with cordon apple and pear trees. The old, well established hedge harboured a great deal of bindweed which I was unable to eradicate because its roots were protected by those of the privet. I used a line of roofing slates, buried vertically in the soil, to prevent the roots of the bindweed growing into the vegetable garden, and I made sure that it did not set seed. These two measures kept the bindweed under control, but I was very pleased when the removal of the hedge finally gave me the opportunity to get rid of it completely.

I pulled out the privet with the aid of a small winch and removed most of the bindweed roots at the same time. Wire netting and steel posts were then used to make a boundary fence before planting the cordon apple and pear trees. Although I tried to remove as much bindweed as possible along with the hedge, many small pieces of root were left in the soil. In order to prevent these fragments sending up shoots to climb the fence, I covered the soil with a sheet of black polythene, slitting it to fit around the posts and trees. Occasionally, I lifted the polythene and pulled out any shoots of bindweed that had grown, to prevent them reaching the light and making food. This method took about 18 months to exhaust the last of the bindweed roots and kill them off.

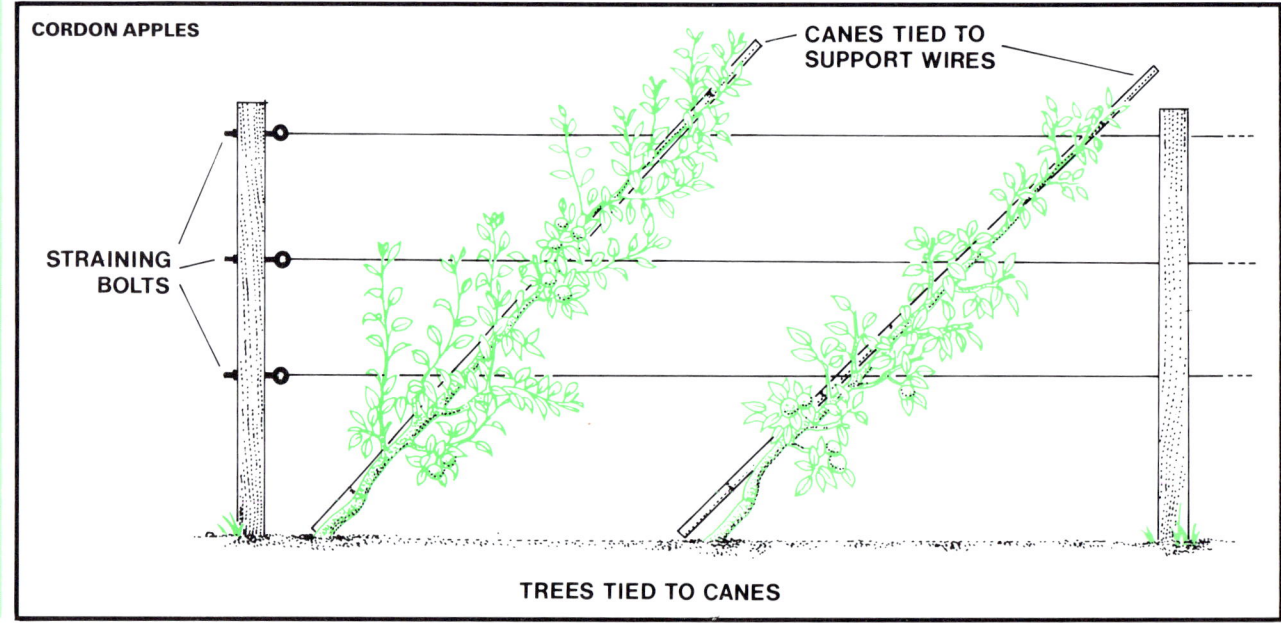

CORDON APPLES

CANES TIED TO SUPPORT WIRES

STRAINING BOLTS

TREES TIED TO CANES

Useful Addresses

Elm Farm Research Centre,
Hamstead Marshall, Berkshire RG15 0HR

Soil analysis service

Henry Doubleday Research Association,
National Centre for Organic Gardening, Ryton-on-Dunsmore,
Coventry CV8 3LG

The Soil Association Ltd,
86-88 Colston Street, Bristol, Avon BS1 5BB

The Soil Association's Symbol scheme acts as a consumer
guarantee of quality. Members receive a free quarterly
magazine which covers subjects such as organic farming, food
quality and dangers of pesticides

Transatlantic Plastics,
Polythene Packaging Division, 23 Brighton Road, Surbiton,
Surrey KT6 5LR

Suppliers of:
Black and clear polythene sheets and other polythene products